POLITICS, DEATH
& ADDICTION

Published by Brolga Publishing Pty Ltd
ABN 46 063 962 443
PO Box 12544
A'Beckett St
Melbourne, VIC, 8006
Australia

email: markzocchi@brolgapublishing.com.au

National Library of Australia Cataloguing-in-Publication entry

Author:	Hirsh, Carolyn
Title:	Politics, death and addiction : a powerful story of a mother's reaction to her daughter's suicide / Carolyn Hirsh.
ISBN:	9781922175458 (paperback)
Subjects:	Hirsh, Carolyn.
	Politicians--Australia--Biography.
	Mothers of suicide victims--Australia--Biography.
	Mothers and daughters--Australia--Biography.
Dewey Number:	324.2092

Printed in Adelaide
Cover design by Chameleon Print Design
Typeset by Wanissa Somsuphangsri

BE PUBLISHED

Publish through a successful publisher. National distribution, Macmillan & International distribution to the United Kingdom, North America. Sales Representation to South East Asia
Email: markzocchi@brolgapublishing.com.au

POLITICS, DEATH & ADDICTION

CAROLYN HIRSH

CONTENTS

❖

CHAPTER 1

FIRST TRANSGRESSION

A s I topped the crest of the hill, almost home, my windscreen framed a confusion of blue and red lights. I braked. Ahead of me was a massive van, lit like Christmas. Orange witches' hats directed traffic into the right lane towards a row of police officers. There was so much light I could even see the white tubes sticking out of their breathalyzers. My stomach knotted and I began to shake. Was I over the legal limit of .05? I spotted a side street and made a nifty left turn. Safe, I thought. I was wrong. A siren and an offshoot of the lights pulled up beside me, forcing me to a stop.

I pressed the automatic window opener, turned off the ignition, and sat, tears spilling. The media would love this. I could already see the headline, Member of Parliament caught drink driving. Why had I driven myself home? Why had I not caught a taxi? Why had I gone to the lower house 'chook house' party after the upper house finished? I hid my face in my hands, like a small child who thinks that by covering her face, she is invisible.

I heard a voice, a male voice.

'Do you have a reason for turning into this street ma'am?

I shook my head. Didn't lift it from my hands.

'Blow into this please ma'am.'

I sensed the presence of an arm through the window. I looked up. The police officer's face was blurred through my tears, but the breathalyser didn't move; the white cardboard tube gleamed in front of my lips.

'Please blow into this,' the voice repeated.

I placed my lips around the tube, blew feebly.

'Harder, please ma'am.'

'I can't blow any harder, I have asthma.'

I reached into my handbag and pulled out my Ventolin inhaler. *Perhaps it'll lower the reading*, I thought irrationally. I sucked in two long puffs, held my breath, trying to postpone the inevitable. The copper was still there, holding the tube in front of my face.

'Would you blow into the tube now, please ma'am,' he said.

I blew again. The machine beeped and the police officer pulled it out of the car window and peered at it. The arm was replaced by a face at the window.

'Could I see your licence please ma'am?'

I scrabbled in my bag and handed it over. *Now they'll know who I am.* I watched the police officer's face as he read the name. Impassive? Maybe a slight lift of an eyebrow? He walked to the other side of the car, checked the registration label, and headed to his own Christmas light-decked car. I sat still, feeling sick. Why hadn't I thought about drinking, about the law? I chaired the Drugs and Crime Prevention Parliamentary Committee after all. *Where did my judgment go? What have I done?*

❖

It was Wednesday 2 June 2004, the second last sitting day of the Autumn session, 10.00 pm. I was about eighteen months into a third term as a Member of the Victorian Parliament. I had served two terms between 1985 and 1992 in the Legislative Assembly, and had lost the election when Jeff Kennett's Liberal government swept into power. Ten years later, I was back in Parliament, in the Legislative Council, riding another tidal wave — Steve Bracks' Labor Government. While my election was a surprise, I was soon immersed again in the role of a Member of Parliament, undertaking policy and committee work, representing constituents, and participating in Parliament.

Although the upper house had risen for the night, the Legislative Assembly was sitting late. As I headed for my car, I saw a group of lower house Members having drinks on the verandah of the 'chook house', which housed most of their offices. They were celebrating the end of the Autumn Parliamentary session. Someone waved; that was all I needed, and I headed over to join them. This group of Labor Party Members was different from my Legislative Assembly colleagues of the nineteen eighties and early nineties. There were many more women and they were generally a much younger cohort than we had been. Some of the women even had young children. I enjoyed their company, and I relished their respect for me as an 'elder stateswoman'. I joined them for a drink and stayed too long.

❖

'Would you step out of the car please, Ms Hirsh?' The police officer was back at the car window, still polite, face expressionless. I couldn't step out, osteoarthritis in my left hip meant I clambered from the car, hanging onto the door, like an elderly hippo. *He probably thinks I'm too drunk.* The police officer shepherded me to the bright caravan from which I had tried to flee.

He ushered me to a chair beside a table on which sat some technical looking equipment — a computer? A printer? Another officer took a second breathalyser test, and the equipment spat out a printed reading. It showed me the worst, a blood alcohol concentration (BAC) of .07, .02 above the legal limit. The two officers were very kind.

'I guess you know who I am?' I asked.

'Yes,' the senior one said. 'We have access to all registered cars on the internet.'

'Please don't tell the media.' My tears started again. I didn't realise that a twenty-four hour news cycle meant media outlets had constant access to police activity.

'You'll be given a set penalty,' the officer said. 'You'll receive a letter telling you when you have to stop driving and when you can start again.'

'Can I go now?'

'No,' he said. 'You're over the limit. We'll take you home.'

One officer drove me home, while another followed in my car.

I did not sleep and felt progressively sicker throughout the night as the alcohol wore off, rather than the other way round.

As I drove into Parliament the next morning for the last day of the session, I rang Lisa McDonald, the Caucus liaison officer. Lisa was the person who ensured the Premier and the Media Unit were aware of what was going on among the backbench. With hindsight I wouldn't have rung her; I'd have told no one. Further, I would have headed straight home from Parliament the night before, instead of allowing the 'chook house' party to divert me.

'Is the media saying anything about me?' I asked her.

'Why?'

'Oh, nothing much,' I said in an airy tone.

'What's happened?' she persisted, exactly as she was paid to do.

Of course, I burst into tears and confessed all.

'Oh,' she said. 'I'll ring you back.'

I should clarify that this conversation took place on a hands-free phone in a cradle, which worked through the car radio — I did not compound my criminal activity. The phone rang a few minutes later.

'Yes,' Lisa said. 'The media's aware of you measuring .07 on a breathalyser last night. We're organising a press conference. It's better if you face the lot at once, 'fess up, and get it out of the way.'

I went straight to my Spring Street office when I arrived at Parliament. Someone from the media unit came in and 'prepped' me for the impending press conference. I didn't think I needed a rehearsal. I'd held a number of press conferences over the years. This was different though. As I was leaving, Lisa came in and told me the Premier wanted to see me. I went to his office, reluctantly.

I had known Steve Bracks for years, and had always found him to be friendly and warm. Not this time though, and I couldn't blame him.

'You have to resign from the Drugs and Crime Prevention Committee,' Steve Bracks said.

He was right of course, but I was devastated.

'How about if I just resign as Chair?'

'No,' he said. 'You have to resign from the Committee.'

I was reluctant to agree, although I knew he was right. I

was grateful for the privilege afforded me in serving this term in Parliament, and chairing the Drugs and Crime Prevention Committee was an even greater honour. Our current and future inquiries made for interesting and challenging policy development work. I was desolated at losing the committee, and this loss swirled through the overcast of shame and humiliation from the night before.

'You can possibly go back next year,' the Premier suggested.

It didn't make me feel better.

I took a deep breath and headed out to the garden, where press conferences often took place.

'I'll stand opposite you,' the media adviser said. 'Just look directly at me the whole time.'

My stomach rolled and my heart thumped as we approached the cluster of media. The garden looked fresh and green, not like winter. I took some deep breaths as radio reporters' microphones and recorders were shoved at me. I could see the furry grey television microphones on their long poles, hanging above me like a group of possums. Television cameras eyed me off, and newspaper photographers clicked still shots into being.

My brief was to be contrite, which was easy. I was.

'I went to see the Premier this morning and offered him my resignation from the Drugs and Crime Prevention Committee, which he accepted.'

The cameras followed me to the back door, and I crept inside, horrified at my stupidity, tears leaking.

The Melbourne Herald Sun reported in part the next day:

A tearful Labor MP stood down yesterday as head of Victoria's drugs and crime prevention committee after she was caught drink-driving.

"I've made a massive mistake, so there's no doubt I'm a bloody idiot. And I'll pay for that mistake," Carolyn Hirsh said.

The committee is inquiring into harmful drinking.
Ms Hirsh, 66, said she had two drinks over dinner with friends on Wednesday night, then two glasses of white wine at a Labor Party bash at Parliament...

...She was breathalysed by a booze bus on Burke Rd, Glen Iris, about 11pm and blew .07 – .02 above the limit.

Ms Hirsh, the member for Silvan, said she had learned a valuable lesson that she was unable to metabolise alcohol as quickly as she thought.

"I'm very remorseful. I feel very bad," she said.

The Financial Review chose a more succinct take on my transgression.

Cartoon in the Financial Review Friday 5 June 2004
(Courtesy Financial Review)

Given my law-breaking behaviour, it was appropriate that I resign from the committee. Questions swirled. Why had I driven the night before when I had been drinking? It would have been so easy to call a taxi. In my two earlier terms in the Victorian Parliament, members did not have to think about taxis. It was done for us. Cars weren't provided to backbench members of Parliament then. We drove our own cars, and on nights Parliament sat, Legislative Assembly attendants handed out taxi vouchers to members who wanted them. I didn't drink much or often in those days, but fatigue was a sufficient reason for a voucher. I would enjoy a train trip in to work the following morning.

It seemed that I was mixing up the two terms of Parliament in my head, although this did not explain my public disrespect for the law — the law I was involved with making.

It has only been in the past three years that I have realised I spent years keeping the horror, grief and guilt following my daughter, Vicki's suicide behind a locked door of denial. A problem was that I also hid other crucial qualities behind this door — joy and pleasure, and even worse, values and judgment.

The drink-driving conviction was shameful for my family and me even if I'd not been a Member of Parliament, but we would not have had to face the public attacks that burst from every media outlet in Victoria. I would have been spared the shame and humiliation that followed my public outing. I spoke about Vicki's suicide and the strong effect alcohol has on me, but it sounded flimsy. *Just excuses.* So why was I serving as a Member of the Victorian Parliament at the age of 67, when I should have been leading a quiet life in retirement?

CHAPTER 2

ELECTED: A MISTAKE & A PRIVILEGE

My mobile rang. It was my brother.

'I'm watching the election coverage on the ABC, and they're saying you've won,' he said.

'Rubbish, I can't have won. The seat is safe Liberal.'

'Well, that's what they're saying; I'm only telling you. Put your car radio on.'

'I can't now. I'm cleaning up the polling booth.'

It was 7.15 on Saturday 30 November, the evening of election day, 2002. I was one of the Labor Party candidates for this election, not expected to win.

❖

Six weeks earlier, I'd received a call from an eastern suburbs Labor Party organiser, a member of the Left, my faction.

'We need a candidate for the Legislative Council Province of Silvan,' Les* said. 'Do you want to do it?'

'No thanks,' I answered. 'I have a lot on my plate at the moment.' This was code for the heaving mess somewhere within me.

'It's a safe Liberal electorate, so there's not much of a chance you'll win it, and you don't have to do any work because it's an upper house seat. We just need a name on the ballot paper. Could you help out?'

I knew there was no need for upper house (Legislative Council) candidates to campaign for an election. Lower house (Legislative Assembly) candidates do the work, because lower house electorates are basic units for the Victorian Electoral Commission. When an election is due, the Electoral Commission opens an office in each electorate and allocates about 20 polling booths to each one. Lower house candidates from all parties campaign to spell out policies and raise their profile in their own electorate, while their party organises volunteers to hand out 'how to vote' cards at each polling booth on election day.

The upper house in the Victorian Parliament provides a second layer of Parliamentary representation, like the Senate in Canberra. In 2002, each upper house province covered four lower house electorates, (now each upper house region covers 11 lower house electorates). Voters at the election simply fill in a second ballot paper to elect their upper house candidates, and those votes tend to 'piggy-back' on the lower house votes.

I was in no fit state, mentally or physically, to stand for election as a serious candidate, but I thought it would be alright since I wouldn't have to do much and was unlikely to win; then Les made a comment that decided me.

---

* not his real name

'Michael Dobson* is going to nominate.'

Michael Dobson was an ambitious young Labor Party member, and an enthusiastic participant in Labor's Right faction. The Right faction's social policy positions had become more and more conservative over the years. *What if he won and took his conservative views to the Parliament?*

I sighed. 'Yes, I'd better do it, just in case.'

I went through the familiar nomination process — collected the required dozen signatures from party members and signed the necessary forms. I discovered that a birth certificate had to accompany the nomination.

'I've never needed to produce a birth certificate with my nomination before. Why is it necessary?'

'To ensure you're an Australian citizen,' Les said.

The production of my birth certificate created a whoosh of incredulity through the local Labor Party.

'You can't be 65!'

'I thought you were fifty-something.'

I'd always been coy about my age, and people made assumptions, even as I was trying to downplay an obvious limp.

'Oh well, too late now. You'll need a special dispensation.'

An antiquated rule still operated in the Labor Party banning anyone aged 65 or more from nominating for public office — a rule made redundant by the passing of anti-discrimination laws in the 1980s, so the special dispensation was duly given.

Michael Dobson also nominated, which meant there would be a contest within the party for the selection of the candidate.

In today's Labor Party, there are few preselection ballots. Most decisions about candidates are made by negotiation. Sometimes a high profile candidate is selected following an order from the

---

* not his real name

State or National party office.

Preselection meetings in the Labor Party are known colloquially as 'the last of the great blood sports'. The venue is usually the Council Chamber in Trades Hall, on the corner of Victoria and Lygon Streets, Carlton South. The chamber oozes labour history, with its decorative dark-stained wood, and banks of seats. Whenever I enter, I sense a shivery presence of ghosts of past union leaders, who stood uncompromisingly for the rights of workers. I always feel like raising my fist to the old comrades and singing *Solidarity Forever*.

Candidates for selection make five minute speeches outlining reasons they deserve the votes of the 100 members of the voting panel, despite the fact that numbers have been counted and the outcome is usually known. Michael Dobson spoke first at this contest. In 1980s preselections, when few women nominated for parliamentary positions, there would be subtle — or sometimes overt — derogatory references to gender. Such discrimination was off-limits in 2002, but my age was fair game.

'Carolyn Hirsh is 65,' he said. 'How can she possibly contribute usefully at that age? She should stay in retirement.'

This produced an ominous murmur from older members of the voting panel. When my turn came to speak, I decided on some payback. I gave my opponent a few surreptitious glances to check his physical features. I stood at the podium and said,

'Michael Dobson remarked that I am too old to stand as a Parliamentary candidate. If I were to go down the same path, I could mention that he is too fat, and might suffer high blood pressure or other ailments of too much weight. However, I won't, of course.'

This comment caused sufficient hilarity for the rest of my speech to go largely unheard. I won the preselection contest, and my name went on the ballot paper as the Labor Party candidate for Silvan Province.

❖

On this election night, I'd won the job of turning the Bayswater West Primary School polling booth back into a school ready for Monday morning's students. I'd handed out 'how to vote' cards there all day, because we'd lived in the same street as the school was for twenty years and my daughters had attended the school. I knew many of the people who voted there, and had enjoyed catching up with old acquaintances throughout the day.

As I pulled down the myriad signs, all sporting the smiling face of the lower house Labor candidate for Bayswater, Peter Lockwood, my brother's phone call rolled around in my head. *What if I really had won? What a great opportunity. I can't do it.* I wanted to get to the car to listen to the election broadcast, but the Young Labor members who'd spent hours that morning from about 3.00 am decorating the polling booth had made sure no one would miss Peter Lockwood's face. There was so much stuff!

❖

The frantic embellishment that transforms schools into intimidating advertisements for the political parties contesting elections started in 1992. I still carry the stark picture that greeted me at 7.45 am on election day, 1992. It was my last day as the Member for Wantirna, a position I'd held for seven and a half years. I arrived at my first polling booth, Ferntree Gully

North Primary school, set in a semi-rural environment among eucalypts, at the foot of the Dandenongs, and thought I would be sick.

It looked like a Liberal Party campaign office. My helpers had placed the usual three or four A-frames with identifying posters around the polling booth, but all I could see was a hundred metres of one-metre-wide plastic sheeting, adorned with repetitive pro-liberal and anti-labor motifs. The catchy phrase, *The Guilty Party,* a message attacking Labor, was repeated in garish red and black — the Liberals had been using this slogan effectively in their pre-election advertising. The sheets of plastic had been draped along fences, between trees, on walls, on poles, everywhere I looked. The decorations burned into my eyes and knotted my stomach. I knew then that I would lose that election and I did.

At each election since, the major political parties have decorated polling booths with hundreds of metres of plastic sheeting. It became, and still is, a competition to see who can get there first to secure the spots that voters will see first. The environmental vandalism of the practice horrifies me. *What happens to the kilometres of plastic from all around the State, and worse, the country?* No one asks this question, because neither party is prepared to stop. It is supposed to influence voters who do not make up their minds about how to vote until they arrive at the polling booth.

❖

My car looked like a tradesman's van. The boot and the back seat were crammed with metres of plastic. Some of the poles on which signs had been fixed were so long I had to hang them out the window.

My phone rang again.

'You've definitely won,' my brother said. 'There's no doubt. The ABC says the Labor Party has swept the outer eastern suburbs.'

I was silent. Excited for my lower house colleagues, but *I couldn't do it. I can't even manage my teaching job properly. Can't look after Jessica properly. How can I be a Member of Parliament again?*

I had to visit the lower house candidates. First, I had to deal with the junk in the car. Peter Lockwood's house wasn't far away. It was empty of course. He was closeted somewhere with his campaign director and his family, recording totals of votes from each polling booth as Labor Party scrutineers rang them in.

I dumped my car's contents of plastic, posters and poles on the Lockwood front lawn — I knew Peter would be too excited to mind — and headed to the Bayswater post-election party. As I parked I could hear cheering and laughter from the hall. My entry was greeted with even louder cheers and my stomach clenched into a knot once more. Peter had won the unwinnable election, and so had I.

Melbourne's Eastern and Outer Eastern suburbs are fertile ground for unwinnable elections for Labor. Ambitious Labor apparatchiks are only interested in standing in Melbourne's North and West, and bits of the South, where electorates are safe Labor. Those who stand as candidates in the East are usually hard working local Party members. Every few years, when the cycle of democracy turns another circle, the voters throw out whichever lot is in. Bunches of young new Members come into State or Federal Parliament, and serve a term or two before they lose again. I should have been ecstatic.

❖

I had not won my first unwinnable election, 20 years before. I had wanted to win so much that time. *So different this time.* My cohort had retired. The new lot reminded me of us twenty years before — young, enthusiastic, and most of all, disbelieving. I was certainly not politically naïve this time. I had learned a lot during twenty years of Labor Party politics, in and out of Parliament. I had represented a local community in Parliament and learned how to compromise. As a member of the Left, I had learned factional politics, unpleasant but necessary. I had participated in Federal politics twice, as a candidate for the Federal electorate of La Trobe, and in policy and research positions, working for the late Senator Olive Zakharov and former Senator Barney Cooney. The job of a Member of Parliament should have been a breeze — I possessed a detailed understanding of it, but I was fearful that my election was a mistake, that at this time I could not manage the tasks required of a Member of Parliament. Over the next four years, to my shame and grief, I proved this to be the case.

❖

I trekked in turn to the functions that each of the candidates in Silvan Province, now my province, were holding, to thank party workers and congratulate the bevy of committed new Labor Members of Parliament. I also called at the function of my friend Anne Eckstein, who was the Labor candidate for the lower house electorate of Ferntree Gully.

Over the years that I had been a member of the Labor Party, since the early 1970s, I had attended more election night functions than I could count. The most exciting was in 1972, on December 2, when Gough Whitlam won after 23 years of opposition. The saddest were in 1975, when John Kerr and Malcolm Fraser sacked Gough Whitlam's Labor Government, and in 1992 when Jeff Kennett decimated Victorian Labor and me.

It should have been an exhilarating evening. I was pleased for my excited colleagues, who had worked non-stop for months at the campaign. I kept grief and guilt packed away, and forgot my trepidation about the task ahead. I could not take credit for my win, because it was due in most part to a massive overall swing to Labor. Well run campaigns in the lower house electorates that covered Silvan Province contributed. Dympna Beard won Kilsyth; Monbulk was won by James Merlino, and of course Peter Lockwood won Bayswater. The fourth electorate, Warrandyte, remained in the hands of the Liberal Party, but the Labor candidate, Jarrod Panther, a young man standing for the first time, gained a respectable swing. In Ferntree Gully Anne Eckstein gained a swing towards her of almost ten percent. Ferntree Gully and Bayswater interested me particularly, because between them, they covered most of the lower house electorate of Wantirna where I had been the representative between 1985 and 1992.

Each post-election celebration I attended swarmed with ebullient members of Labor Party branches of Melbourne's Outer Eastern suburbs.

'We haven't had such a fantastic result since John Cain won in 1982.'

'The best night since Hawkie won in 1983.'

'Reminds me of Gough in 1972,' some old-timers of my era shouted.

I arrived home about midnight, sat on the edge of my bed and thought about how impossible it is to predict the future. My mind went back ten years, when I sat on the edge of my bed after I had lost the 1992 election, having served for over seven years. I recalled the painful emotions of losing an election, like being escorted from my workplace by a security guard. Sacked without notice. I couldn't believe I was back in parliament. I should have been overjoyed, but I was emotionally blank.

My eldest daughter Vicki had committed suicide twenty months before, and I had not begun to grieve. I could not face the horror, so I had kept the agony locked down somewhere. This meant that other emotions were inaccessible to me as well. I felt as if I was living in a brittle, distant place. I should be able to deal with her death. It's not the first. Look at all the others. My thoughts drifted.

CHAPTER 3
FIRST DEATH -
THE AVALANCHE BEGINS

'There's a typhoon in Hong Kong. Thirty-five inches of rain and landslides. Someone's dead. The news says it's Kevin Murphy.'

My 14 year-old stepson, Michael, stood in the bedroom doorway. He was pale.

'Coincidence,' I said. 'There must be two people called Kevin Murphy in Hong Kong.'

The younger of my two brothers was Kevin Murphy, and he was at that time a journalist with the *South China Morning Post*, an English language newspaper in Hong Kong. Of course it wouldn't be him. He was my brother. *Anyway, we would have heard if anything had happened to Kevin.*

It was the Queen's birthday holiday, 13 June 1966, seven in the morning. Grey, drizzling. I didn't care much about the queen, but it felt good to snuggle under the blankets. No need to get up — no school lunches, no hurry. My husband, Peter, had left at six to open our garage — black night, no stars, no moon. I didn't need to go in though. It was a long weekend for me. We'd bought the business a year before, and Peter worked long and hard on the petrol pumps as we built it up. We only employed one mechanic — did the rest ourselves, including in those days, full driveway service for every customer who bought petrol. Peter would run all day as more and more customers came to us — he'd prop the pump in the tank, and as the petrol poured in he'd wash the windscreens, check the air pressure in the tyres and open the bonnet to check and top up the oil and water. He'd sell oil and windscreen wipers and anything else the customer wanted. He smiled and joked with the men, who generally got out of their cars and watched. He was courteous to the women who wound down their windows but stayed put. I did the books, the accounts, the ordering and cleaning. All hard work, but worth it.

❖

I was concerned enough about this Kevin Murphy being dead, despite my disbelief, to crawl out of bed and put the 'wireless' on for the 7.30 news-in-brief. I heard someone say it. It was the first item.

'Kevin Murphy, 23, an Australian journalist with the *South China Morning Post,* was killed yesterday as a typhoon hit Hong Kong. He was one of at least two Europeans to perish.'

Kevin was 23 years old. He would be 24 in a month.

I have to find out what's going on.

I rang the radio station that had twice broadcast the item.

'Why are you broadcasting this nonsense? My brother is Kevin Murphy, and we know nothing of this.'

'We received the information from the wire at the *Sydney Daily Telegraph*,' the person on duty said. 'He used to work there.'

My stomach churned. Kevin had worked at the *Sydney Daily Telegraph* until he'd gone to Hong Kong nine months previously.

I rang the Sydney paper. Eventually Bob* came to the phone. He was a friend of Kevin's whom I'd met.

'Hasn't anyone told you?' He sounded shocked.

'No, I've just heard a news report on the radio. It can't be true.'

'I'm afraid it is. The police found Kevin's body in the mud near the peak tramline. He and John Stuart, the deputy night editor, had been trying to drive up to John's place at the peak. John's wife is pregnant and he was worried about her with the reports of all the landslides. They were both washed off a bridge over the tramline. There were massive rocks from the landslides higher up.'

'How can you be sure it's Kevin?' I was in a horror of disbelief.

'John Ryan** went to the morgue and identified his body.' John Ryan was another friend.

I thought I would vomit or faint. Trembled. My first serious state of shock.

'We don't know. Why hasn't anyone told us? My parents don't know. My brother and his wife are driving home from Mildura this morning. They might smash their car if they hear it on the news.'

'All the lines out of Hong Kong have been down for nearly 24 hours. It's been chaos, but we got a message overnight from AAP.'

---

*, **   Not their real names

'Bob, can you please get it off the news. I have to tell my mother and brother.'

'I'm sorry, I'm sorry,' he said. *Sorry? What does sorry mean? A string of sounds.*

'I'll get it off the news bulletins straight away,' he said.

'I've got to tell Mother.' I was alternately screaming and howling by this stage.

I can't ring her. I have to go there.

We only had one car then, and Peter had taken it to work. I didn't want to worry him with it yet. It was probably a mistake. I grabbed *The Age* from the letterbox. My hands shook so much I could hardly hold it. *Nothing on the first page, or the second or third. Oh God. In the centre of page four.*

The Age, Monday June 13, 1966

Melbourne man dies in deluge

HONG KONG, June 12. — A Melbourne journalist was among more than 100 known dead and injured in a freak deluge which gave the colony one of its wettest and blackest Sundays.

The journalist was Mr. Kevin Murphy, 24, a subeditor of the "South China Morning Post."

A "Post" executive said Murphy was from Melbourne but did not know his home address or family details.

At one stage during the deluge the authorities announced they could not answer any call for aid unless it involved saving lives.

Things became so critical at one stage that the authorities announced they could not answer any call for aid unless it involved saving lives.

Rescue workers feared the toll might be higher as reports of landslides and house collapses filtered in from areas cut off from normal communications and traffic.

The torrential downpours lasted, with few intermissions, from yesterday morning to this evening.

Officially, Hong Kong Island was worse hit than the more densely populated Kowloon mainland.

Twenty-one of the 26 confirmed dead were on the island.

They included three Europeans, one of whom was identified as Tommy Keenan, 11-year-old son of a British Army sergeant.

Initial reports listed 44 people missing and feared killed. Another 29 were injured.

Police, ambulance and fire-engine sirens screamed throughout the day as the colony assumed the appearance of a disaster area.

The 15 inches of rain that fell turned roads into mud rivers and farmland into lakes, flooded shops and houses, and caused landslides and house collapses.

❖

Why hasn't anyone told us? I rang Peter and told him.

'I'd say they've made a mistake,' he said. You'd have been told if it was Kevin. Get a taxi to your mum's place. I'll try to get someone to cover for me. I'll be there as soon as I can.'

I rang a taxi and left our two daughters, aged six and two in the care of my stepchildren, who were 14 and 12. *Kevin always calls Vicki 'the baby', so when Teresa arrived she became 'the little baby'.*

Mother won't have today's papers yet. Father will bring them home about ten. I hope he hasn't read anything.

I got the taxi to stop at the milk bar, and bought a *Sun*. Jerked the pages over. *Page four again.*

Paqe 4 — The Sun, Monday. June 13. 1966

HONGKONG DELUGE KILLS 26

HONGKONG, Sun., AAP.— *Hongkong suffered more than 100 known dead and injured in a freak deluge which turned the colony into a disaster area.*

Among the 26 known dead was Kevin Murphy, 24, a newspaper sub-editor who came from Melbourne.

Rescue workers feared the toll might be higher as reports of landslides and house collapses filtered in from cut-off areas.

The torrential downpour lasted, with few intermissions, from yesterday morning to this evening.

Fifteen inches of rain turned roads into mud, rivers and farmland into lakes, flooded shops and houses, and caused landslides and house collapses.

Rescue operations were hampered by a nearly total breakdown in communications and traffic.

Police said that the entire Victoria Peak area, where more than 50,000 live in hundreds of high-rise luxury apartments, was isolated by landslides and cliff-side breakways.

Police broadcast warnings that scores of streets and roads throughout the colony were in danger of giving away or being hit by landslides.

❖

It was just on eight o'clock when I arrived at my parents' place to tear their lives apart. I couldn't believe it was only been an hour since mine had been shredded. Father wasn't there. He ran the Malvern railway station kiosk each weekday morning from first train until the end of peak time, about 9 am — it kept him in beer money. He would then go off to the pub for a couple of early morning 'heart starters'.

Mother was home of course, because it was a public holiday. She was still in her dressing gown reading her way through her pile of last week's *Ages,* with a cup of tea beside her. She always got behind with the papers during the week as she worked at the local newsagent — it kept them in food money. I had the current papers under my arm.

I can't remember what I said to my Mother, or how I said it or how she reacted. I do remember ringing the *Age* and the *Sun* and asking them to remove the article from later editions, since if this *was* my brother, the family hadn't been told.

I managed to find the number for the *South China Morning Post,* but there was no answer.

'I think the lines might still be down. No calls got through either way yesterday or last night,' the telephone operator told me. 'And remember it's only 6.45 am there.'

'Can you try to get through to the main police station in Hong Kong?' I asked.

Someone answered that call.

'There are broadcasts that a journalist called Kevin Murphy was killed in the tropical downpour yesterday.' My voice shook. My hands shook. My stomach churned. My heart belted so hard I thought it would jump out through my head.

'Yes, that is the case,' the voice on the other end said.

'I have a brother called Kevin Murphy,' I said. 'He's a journalist at the *South China Morning Post*. My family and I don't know anything about it.'

I thought he sounded shocked, but it was not a very good line. 'We didn't have any knowledge of a family; his work colleague and friend and his fiancé identified his body.'

Relief flooded through me. It wasn't Kevin. He wasn't engaged.

'What are their names and telephone numbers please?'

He told me, and I sank back into horror. I knew both. I'd met his friend. They'd worked together at the *Age*. His 'fiancé' was the girlfriend Kevin had told me about in his last letter. 'Just about over her, and I'm about to call it all off.'

The police officer was full of apologies. 'All the lines have been down until a couple of hours ago. We've been without power too.'

I think my mother spoke to him, and we wrote down the phone numbers.

Looking back 46 years to the nature of communication in 1966, the changes between then and now are astonishing. Even the fax machine had just been invented, and was not in general use. Newspapers of course, had telex machines, and that was how the item about Kevin's death appeared in the Melbourne newspapers, via the AAP telex, before we found out.

I remember my mother, in shock, telling my father when he arrived home. She hadn't finished dressing and was in her underwear, but I don't think either of them noticed. There was no way we could tell my other brother until he and my sister-in-law arrived back from Mildura.

I don't recall the day as a timeline, but as a series of events that jump from my memory when I search through it. I arranged for a friend to bring the children to my mother's. Peter arrived at some stage. We eventually spoke by phone to officials in Hong Kong, who said there was another Kevin Murphy in Hong Kong, and I remember a sliver of hope for a short time, but confirmation came after a while that it was our Kevin Murphy. My mother said he could be buried there.

'It would cost too much to bring his body home,' she said. 'None of us has the money.'

'I have to see him.' I was insistent.

I said if that was to be the case, I was going immediately to attend his funeral. In the end, she agreed that we would bring his body home. More phone calls to and from Kevin's friends, to the police, to senior staff at the paper, led to an offer to pay the costs of returning his body home — it may have come from the Hong Kong government.

I rang Alan and Lyn (my older brother and sister-in-law) once they arrived home from their long weekend in Mildura. I suppose my mother or I rang the rest of the family. There was a big family in 1966. Each of my parents had seven brothers and sisters and most of them were still around. My mother's brother, Joe, had died just six weeks earlier.

My brother, Kevin Murphy

❖

Kevin's body arrived about a week-and-a half after his death, and was at the funeral parlour awaiting the funeral. The only dead body I'd ever seen was my cat's. It died when I was about twelve, somewhere about the time my grandfather also died.

I can't remember who else came to see Kevin's body, but I was shocked to recognise him. He looked like a marble statue of himself surrounded by the white satin lining of the coffin. *It is definitely Kevin.* He was dead.

❖

We buried Kevin at Cheltenham New Lawn Cemetery, because that was where my uncle Joe had been buried two months earlier. The cemetery became a familiar place over the next seven years.

We buried my father in the grave with Kevin in June 1969, followed a year later by my grandmother in a new grave. She died on July 20, Kevin's birthday, of a quick stroke after a good win at the races. In May 1971, my cousin Ross, a year younger than me, died suddenly in Hobart. There was room for him in his father, Joe's grave. Ross and I had grown up together. He was more like a brother than a cousin.

The avalanche of death roared loudly in October 1973, when my husband Peter died. He's at Cheltenham too.

CHAPTER 4
PETER'S DEATH

My husband, Peter Hirsh died on October 15, 1973, of herpes simplex encephalitis, (HSV–1). I was 36, and it was the worst three weeks I'd ever experienced. The disease was not diagnosed properly until after his death, when the virus had eaten most of his brain. In recent years, an anti-viral treatment has become available, but nothing could be done then. Medicine has come a long way in 40 years. Ninety percent of people carry this virus — it causes cold sores, but usually does not develop into a disease. A compromised immune system may be the culprit that allows the virus to invade the brain, and that's what I believe happened to Peter.

We'd bought a Shell service station franchise in 1965, a run-down business in Bennettswood. I looked after the books and money, and Peter worked long hours to build up the business. In the early days, he spent many of these hours serving petrol, until we could afford to employ staff — this was well before the days of 'self-serve' petrol.

'Check your oil, Sir?' Peter would ask as he cleaned the windscreen. The customer generally stayed in the car, like McDonalds drive through now.

However, petrol contained lead in those days, and I believe Peter's exposure to lead in the petrol compromised his immune system.

His illness and death ran like a black and white horror movie for almost three weeks, some of which I cannot recall, while stark shards of the events still flick through my mind at times.

Peter came home from work one Wednesday with a shocking headache and fever.

He went to the doctor and received a penicillin injection.

'Flu,' the doctor said.

'Yes, flu,' we said.

Peter

We had little idea in those days of the difference between a viral and bacterial infection, and the uselessness of antibiotics for the former. It seems, looking back, that the doctor could not differentiate either.

Peter stayed in bed the next day, Thursday, and I went to the garage and spoke to our mechanic.

'The boss has the flu quite badly. He'll be off sick all next week. Can you manage for the week? I'll do the till each day.'

I rang the casuals and booked them in for extra shifts. Later I drove Peter back to the doctor for the second of the course of three antibiotic injections, which didn't seem to be helping. He went to work on the Friday morning, but arrived home a couple of hours later. His face looked as if it were coated with white flour. He was nauseated and had such a headache its intensity may have been approaching that of childbirth contractions. He fell into bed and stayed there. The doctor came at my insistence and gave him tablets for the pain and another antibiotic injection.

'A very bad attack of flu,' he said. 'He should show signs of improvement by tomorrow.'

Despite the painkillers, Peter's headache did not improve. He could not eat or drink and the nausea increased. By midday Saturday, I became frightened. I rang the doctor and discovered there was a locum on duty.

I need to do something,' I said. 'He can't even get out of bed, and he can't bear the headache.'

'You'd better bring him to the surgery. You can come straight away.'

It did not occur to me to ring an ambulance. Perhaps nearly 40 years ago, it was not a usual thing to do or perhaps I just did not know about it. I helped Peter out of bed and into his dressing gown. He leaned on me while we got to the car, and managed somehow to sit in the front seat. My middle daughter Teresa's last memory of her father is a picture of him leaning on me as we headed to the car.

The locum took Peter's temperature — it was nearly 40°C — and he conducted a simple test, which had not occurred to our family doctor over the previous three days. He asked Peter to bend his head forward, to try to touch his chin to his chest. As he attempted this, he moaned in agony.

'I think he has meningitis,' the doctor said. 'He'll have to go to Fairfield Infectious Diseases Hospital. Can you take him? '

Already in shock over Peter's debilitation, I said 'Yes,' but I was concerned that my old car would bump him about too much.

'I'll have to get the other car. I can't take him in this one, and I've left the children at home on their own. I have to arrange for someone to look after them.'

The doctor did not suggest calling an ambulance, which now would have seemed the appropriate thing to do, and the idea still didn't occur to me.

A morphine injection gave Peter immediate relief, so I left him to sleep for the first time for more than twenty-four hours in the doctor's surgery. I went home, dropped the three girls at a neighbour's place, and swapped cars from my 10-year-old poorly sprung Holden to our almost new, smooth-as-silk Ford.

The trip to Fairfield was uneventful since Peter was pain-free and only half-awake. Or half-conscious? When we arrived, nursing staff bundled him into a wheelchair and took him away. I sat on a chair in a waiting room for hours, I have no idea how many. Finally a medical person, doctor or nurse — it could have been the cleaner for all I knew — came into the room.

'There's no point you waiting any longer dear,' they said to me. 'We are still doing tests to see what's going on and it will take a while yet. He is comfortable and not in any pain. Why don't you go home and ring us in the morning. We should have results of the tests by then.'

The hospital could not ring me at home, as we had no

telephone. We had sold our previous house a few months earlier and were living in a nearby rental house, which we colloquially labeled 'the dump'. Our new dream home was almost complete, only about three weeks off. We hadn't bothered getting a phone connected at 'the dump' as we had a work phone, and there was a public telephone box across the road — no mobiles in those days.

So, I went home. The only thing I remember about the Saturday night is staying up all night in a frenzy of washing every washable item in the house — bedding, clothing, crockery cutlery, and wiping every surface with disinfectant. I was afraid that if Peter had meningitis, the children might catch it, and I couldn't sleep.

I rang the hospital from the public phone the next morning, and got through to the nurse in charge of Peter's ward.

'He's had a comfortable night, and he is not in any pain at the moment. He is quite sleepy,' she told me.

'But what's wrong with him?' I asked. 'Can I come out and see him now?'

'You'll need to talk to the doctor about the test results. I'm not allowed to discuss them,' she said. 'The doctor who is looking after him will be in after lunch. Come in then and you can visit your husband, and talk to the doctor.'

As I dredge the details from my memory to write about the horror of this time, I can't believe how acquiescent I was toward the nurses and doctors who were caring for my husband. Why had I not insisted on staying at the hospital the previous day? Why had I not insisted on speaking to a doctor when I rang up on the Sunday morning?

I went to Fairfield straight after lunch to visit Peter. A neighbour drove us all to the hospital, but the children weren't allowed in. It was hospital policy. Why? The culture of the time? Because it was an infectious diseases hospital? Teresa remembers the three girls had to sit in the car for an hour with our neighbour, while I 'visited'. They did not see their father again after I drove him to the doctor's on the Saturday.

Peter was sleepy and nauseated, although his headache had gone. We talked a little, but he kept dozing off. I managed to find a doctor.

'Your husband has viral meningitis,' he told me. 'It means a virus has attacked the meninges, which are protective membranes that surround and protect the brain and spinal cord.'

'Will he be all right?' I asked.

'Yes,' the doctor said. 'It is a serious illness and he will be in hospital for about 10 days, but he will recover fully.'

I can still dredge up the flood of relief that washed through my body when the doctor told me that Peter would be all right. I had been terrified he would die. From recent tragedies that had occurred I was no longer immune to the possibility of death of someone close. The comfortable cocoon of, 'it can't happen to me' had disappeared seven years before when my journalist brother, Kevin, was accidently killed in a Hong Kong cyclone, at the age of 23 years. The sudden death of my cousin Ross, a year younger than me, in 1971 dragged me further out of that belief. Also in the seven years between 1966 and 1973 an uncle, my father and my grandmother had died. I knew death *could* happen, because it had.

❖

I slept well on the Sunday night. I took the children to school early Monday morning, arrived at work at about 9.00 o'clock, and rang the hospital. The switchboard put me straight through to the ward.

'How is my husband? Is he any better yet?' I asked.

'We've been trying to get in touch with you for hours Mrs. Hirsh.' Your husband does not have viral meningitis. He began having fits during the night, so the illness must be within the brain. We don't know what it is, the doctors are with him now. Could you come to the hospital please?'

I fell straight back into shock. Fits? What was wrong?

At the hospital a doctor expanded on what the nurse had said.

'The tests we did were positive for a virus, which is why we assumed viral meningitis. However, the seizures change that picture, and we don't know exactly what he has,' the doctor said. 'We're doing more tests, and he's gone downstairs for x-rays — he may have a tumor in the brain. His temperature is still very high, and we are trying to bring it down, as well as giving him medication to try to stop the seizures.'

❖

My next memory is of sitting with Peter later that day, after he was back in a ward. He seemed much better. His headache was gone, he no longer felt sick, and he was quite talkative for the first time since he became ill. But, as we talked, fear flicked through my body as I realised that much of what he was saying did not make sense. I left him to find a doctor, but couldn't, and I burst into tears as I tried to explain my fear to a nurse. I remember her being reassuring.

'He has a very high fever, he's probably delirious,' she said.

Leaving the hospital in time to pick up the children, I packed necessities and drove to my mother's place to stay, as she had a telephone. I felt in need of support, as I was frightened of the symptoms and Peter's prognosis.

The next day, I took the children to school, called at the garage, and headed for Fairfield. The hospital had not rung, so I hoped the whole thing was a bad dream and I would find Peter sitting up in bed sipping on a cup of tea while we talked rationally.

Not so. He had been moved to a small room, with windows facing onto the nurses' station. I asked why.

'He's extremely ill, and we need to keep him under observation,' a nurse said. 'He's very sleepy, but I'm sure he'd like you to sit with him.'

I went in, but Peter did not seem to register my presence. He had a drip going into his arm, and a catheter. His only covering was a sheet, and his lips looked blue. I went out and asked a nurse for a blanket for him.

'He looks as though he's cold.'

'No,' she said. He has a high fever, and has ice packs around him. We must bring his temperature down.'

I sat by the bed for a long time, holding his hand, stroking his forehead and talking to him. I have no recollection of what I might have said. He occasionally looked at me and murmured some words, which I could not make out. I finally told him I had to leave, to pick up the children from school. I kissed him, turned to leave. He cried out, tried to get out of bed, scattering tubes and ice, and ended up collapsed on the floor. Nurses rushed in, one escorted me from the room, and the door and blinds on the window were closed. I was locked out, and did not see my husband conscious again.

I sat for a long time, until someone told me I should go home, which I did.

Later the hospital rang me at my mother's place to tell me Peter had lost consciousness and they were unable to arouse him. My memories of the next ten days are flashes, out of sequence, like the old black-and-white movie with the projector breaking down constantly. A doctor informed me that Peter could not breathe on his own, and had been placed in a negative pressure ventilator, that is an 'iron lung'. An 'iron lung' or tank respirator, forces the body to breathe when it cannot do it for itself. An airtight metal tank encloses all of the body except the head and forces the lungs to inhale and exhale through regulated changes in air pressure. The modern tracheotomy tube and ventilation system have replaced the iron lung and comparable respirators of the past.

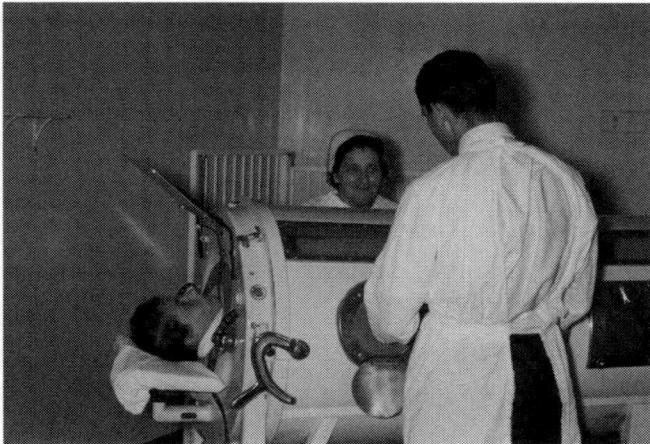

A patient in an 'iron lung' (Courtesy Wikimedia Commons).

I arranged for the oil company to provide a short-term manager, and spent each day sitting next to Peter, who remained still and silent in the 'iron lung'. The only sounds were the rush of air into the pump and the quiet humming of the machine that drove it.

Someone told me that Peter may not recover. That was all the information I could glean. I asked to see a doctor, to try to find out what was wrong with my husband, and for a number of days I was told that doctor was not available, and that the nurses were unable to give me any information. I was finally insistent enough, and was given an appointment. I sat in a visitor's chair in the doctor's office facing him across an enormous desk.

'What's wrong?' I asked. 'Will he get better?' 'Why can't you wake him up?'

The doctor blew smoke from his cigarette into my face as he explained that they had done tests to see whether he had a brain tumour and it wasn't that.

'We think he may have encephalitis. Meningitis is inflammation of the meninges surrounding the brain,' the doctor explained, 'and encephalitis is inflammation of the brain itself.'

'Will he recover?' I asked.

'He has a lot of brain damage, which is permanent and it's unlikely that he will recover.'

'Is he going to die?' I asked.

'He may,' the doctor said. 'Even if he doesn't he is likely to remain in a permanent vegetative state, since the damage to his brain is so severe.'

The three girls were still not allowed into the hospital, but Peter's brother, Brian brought their father in. My father-in-law, Jimmy, sat on a chair and sobbed. No Australian veneer of toughness was necessary for him — he was European, and allowed to show his emotions.

My stepdaughter, Chrissie was allowed to visit because at nineteen she was an adult, as was my stepson, Michael, who was two years older. He happened to be AWOL from the navy at the time, so I rang the navy to inform them of his father's condition. A few hours later, my stepson arrived at the hospital, escorted by a couple of burly military police. It would have been quite funny if it hadn't been so horrible.

Another day when I went to the hospital, as I did each day, I found I could not get near my husband — screens were pulled around and there was a great deal of activity. A nurse asked me to wait. After some time a doctor arrived and said that my husband's heart had stopped beating, but they had managed to start it again.

'He has a very strong heart,' the doctor said

'Doesn't he have severe brain damage?' I asked. 'What's the point of starting his heart if his brain doesn't work?'

'We are legally obliged to treat him in whatever way we can, or we may be found negligent,' the doctor replied.

This episode among others during Peter's illness illustrates the progress that has been made in 40 years in treatment of people whose brain function has ceased. The only criterion for pronouncing a person dead in those days was that the heart had stopped. Brain death could not be used to pronounce death. Those were the days before organ transplants as well.

The last few days of Peter's life after the doctor delivered his news to me are a blur. Doctors started his heart twice more after it stopped beating. On Sunday night, 14 October, our middle daughter, Teresa's ninth birthday, the nurses told me that my husband was likely to die within the next few hours. It seemed to me that it would not make much difference, since for some days he had looked as though he was already dead. Peter 'died', that is his heart stopped beating finally early on Monday morning 15 October.

The doctors asked if they could undertake an autopsy, as their findings would provide information about this extremely unusual condition, and be of great benefit to medicine. I agreed, and this, plus the knowledge that Peter would have been in a 'chronic vegetative state' had he lived provided some comfort to me in the early days of shock and disbelief.

CHAPTER 5
SINGLE PARENT FAMILY

'**S**orry Carolyn. We don't franchise to women.'

I was stunned. I argued, but to no avail. Nick*, the Shell Oil Company Representative, who had been very good to me during the three weeks of Peter's illness, stymied my future with that one short sentence. When I look back over almost forty years, I see how far the law has advanced in relation to discrimination against women. Like changes in health service delivery, the position of women in society has improved dramatically.

Our daughters, Vicki, Teresa and Belinda were aged twelve, nine and five when he died, and we were three weeks short of moving into the 'dream home' we had designed together, and which was nearly complete. Amidst the shock of Peter's death, I had to work out where we would live and what we would live on. We had been due to sign the mortgage and insurance

---

* Not his real name

documents the week after Peter became ill. By then he had suffered a series of seizures and was in a coma.

'Sorry Carolyn,' the bank manager said. 'We don't loan money to women.'

Luckily, my Uncle Jack was a bank manager, and helped me sort out that problem. I signed up under the bank manager's disapproving gaze, and we had a home to move into. Our 'dream home', which had given us such pleasure designing, became my nightmare home.

We moved into our almost complete house two days after Peter's funeral, on a miserable drizzling day. The 'garden' comprised a clay filled building site made wet, slippery and sticky by the constant rain. Inside were new freshly laid carpets. My friend Jillian* and her husband turned up to help us, and we lay a path of 'lilo' mattresses, sugar bags and old mats from the moving truck to the front door.

The owner of the rental property we moved from created another glitch for me. We had kept the rental place in good order during the three months we lived there, but when the owner called to pick up the keys after the movers had gone, he refused to give me back the bond.

He climbed into his car and started the motor, shouting that he had seen some marks on the walls. I raced to his car and perched on the bonnet, shaking.

'I'm not moving until you give me the bond,' I said.

'No, get off,' he replied.

The standoff, or 'sit-off' lasted about half an hour — no mobile phones of course. He finally reached into his pocket, pulled out some notes and handed them to me. I counted them, found they totalled the correct amount, and climbed off the

* Not her real name

bonnet.

❖

I decided early on that I would keep the service station. I understood the business, and the figures showed that I would be able to employ a manager to organise the petrol and the workshop, while I continued with staff and financial management. The income would be sufficient to pay the mortgage and bring up the children, and my hours would be flexible enough so I could be home when they were.

Nick's ultimatum sent me spiralling into new waves of shock, and the fear, my companion over the last weeks, sat on me like lumps of rock. What could I do?

I was a special education teacher by profession, a teacher of children with intellectual disabilities. I had loved it, but had only worked in that field for eighteen months, at two thirds of the male wage. Of course, when I married in 1959 I had to resign, since the Education Department did not employ married women. I was able to continue working as a casual employee at the same school, doing the same job for even less money, for another year until the principal called me into his office one day.

'Are you having a baby?' he asked.

'Yes,' I said, with some pride. 'In four months.'

'You'll have to leave. It's starting to show.'

That was the end of my teaching career.

❖

Nick brought me back to the conversation, which I was having trouble listening to.

'I spoke to some of your friends at Peter's funeral,' he said.

'There's a job waiting for you at Dandenong Special School.'

I was stunned. A couple of lecturers in special education at Burwood Teachers' College and Monash University had been at the funeral, as had some of my teacher friends.

'You'll need to start in two weeks so you'll qualify to be paid over the school holidays,' Nick went on. 'Ring Professor Rogers,* it's all arranged.'

Two weeks later, I started work at Dandenong Special School, in the junior department with two experienced teachers, with six weeks to go before a six week paid break. I had been sent to Dandenong partly because of the school's principal. I was grateful for that. Grace Heaney was kind to me and tolerant of my ignorance of modern teaching theory and practice. For example, I was puzzled when introduced to the terms visual perception and auditory perception. I eventually worked out they were the activities we had called reading and listening in the 1950s.

I was able to become a permanent teacher, since the law preventing married women working was repealed in 1966, with Australia being the last country to repeal this law — although of course, I was no longer a married woman, and would have qualified for permanency under the old rules. Equal pay for women had been introduced the previous year.

The six weeks until the holidays were a blur, exacerbated by my doctor's prescription of one of the ubiquitous benzodiazepines — fashionable at the time — to help me through the days and nights. Neither the doctor nor I

* Not his real name

were aware of the dangers of these drugs, particularly when taken over time. They helped dull the boiling emotions that threatened to incapacitate me, and of course, prevented me from going through an inevitable grief process.

I recall attending a medical examination as part of the process required to become a permanent teacher. As I stood in my underwear, the doctor looked me up and down and asked,

'What are those bruises? Do you drink?'

I did not drink in those days, and I followed the direction of her eyes to my legs. About half way between knees and thighs, there was a mass of bruises, ranging in colour from fresh purple to faded yellow. I was horrified, but realized I had received them by bumping into the corners of children's classroom tables as I walked around the room. I did not tell the doctor about the benzodiazepines, but cut them back.

Those six weeks were difficult for my children, as well as for me. My mother helped a lot, stayed half the week, and took Belinda, the youngest, to and from kindergarten. Vicki had to make her own way to high school, and Teresa walked by herself quite a distance to and from her primary school. She was only in grade 3. Her new school at the top of our new street was not due to open until the following year.

The six weeks holiday helped make up for the hard time we had all experienced. The service station was sold. I sold our powerful car and our caravan, because I did not believe I could manage them on my own, or that I could afford to run the car. I reasoned that if we could no longer enjoy our wonderful caravan holidays, at least the girls could have fun at home, so I installed an in-ground pool. I hoped the pool, at a time when backyard pools were rare, would help counter the disadvantage I felt the children would suffer as part of a 'single parent family.'

The pool turned out to be a good investment, and was a great success through my daughters' childhood and teenage years.

The Principal called me into her office toward the end of my first six-week stint.

'You know your qualifications are out of date, and are inadequate for a teaching career,' she said. 'You need four years training these days. You can do your fourth year through the Education Department.'

'Do I have to decide now?'

'No,' You'll need to enroll at the beginning of the school year.'

The holidays gave me a chance to think about it. The Education Department qualification was only recognized 'in-house', and I had not completed matriculation (year 12) at school. I was dubious about undertaking a qualification that was only of value in the Victorian Education Department.

An advertisement in *The Age* solved my dilemma. One evening in January, feeling lonely and sad, the children in bed, hearing cars pass and wishing one would stop and a visitor would call, I saw an advertisement for 'Adult Higher School Certificate, (now VCE) evening classes.' If I did that, perhaps I could go to university, I thought. I enrolled, and a new vista opened.

The classes, from 7.00 pm to 10.00 pm three evenings a week, did not interfere with work or children. Chrissie, my twenty-year-old stepdaughter, and her friends were willing babysitters. The year had three major outcomes. First, I gained my HSC, second, I was accepted into an Arts degree at Monash University, to major in English and History, and third, most importantly, I received a special distinction in English.

My HSC results shone through my life like a shaft of

summer sun. I was clever, after all.

I still call my university degree 'Gough's gift'. The Whitlam Labor Government provided free tertiary education in 1974, so along with thousands of women who had been denied university because they were girls, and because the cost of tertiary education without a Commonwealth scholarship or a teaching studentship was unaffordable, I leapt into it. It was like jumping out of a plane, or abseiling down a cliff, with plenty of fear, but fizzing excitement.

I continued to teach at Dandenong Special School full-time, and completed English and Sociology at university the first year. I chose those subjects simply because the lectures and tutorials were after school hours. My mother's help was as crucial as Gough's, since she cared for the children and prepared dinner the two evenings I had lectures. I did very well, with a distinction for Sociology and a credit for English. I was grateful for the design of the Menzies building as well, since at times, the 11 floors of escalators kept my children entertained while I attended a late afternoon lecture.

❖

Weaving through the activity in the months after Peter's death were tears, more from the three girls than from me. I can remember feeling anger, despair and guilt, but didn't cry much. One day, a few months after Peter's death, overwhelmed with anger, I gathered all his photographic equipment and sold the lot. As well, I experienced an unpleasant feeling I couldn't identify for eighteen months — it was fear.

Around the middle of 1975, I had to face the fact that I was depressed and had not grieved properly. I had continued to take valium intermittently throughout the eighteen months, and I believe it contributed to suicidal feelings I experienced at that time. The crisis came when I stood on the top floor of the 11 storey 1960s Menzies Arts building the — Ming wing — at Monash, thinking I would like to jump out the window. I did not, and contacted my brother and my family doctor. I spent two weeks in a specialist ward at the Austin hospital, where I was allowed no medication, not even an aspirin. I participated in group therapy, occupational therapy, music therapy, art therapy and relaxation therapy, all of which encouraged me to acknowledge my loss of Peter. I was able to stop being strong, and start recovering from my loss. I missed a total of a month at work, and developed new strength and resilience. I became far closer to the person I wanted to be.

❖

I wanted to be a psychologist. The Monash psychology department ran a two-year psychology program in the Arts department, although a psychology major of three years was only available as a science degree. First and second-year arts students would wander around co-opting 'naïve' students to act as subjects in experiments.

I agreed to participate in a replication of Solomon Asch's ubiquitous demonstration of conformity, the process of giving in to real or imagined pressure from a group. It is a powerful experiment, which I describe here in full because it had a profound effect on my future. The experimenter directed me to sit in a spot towards the end of a row of six other people, whom

I believed to be subjects as well. In fact, they were accomplices of the experimenter. We had to look at a series of pairs of cards, one with a single line and the second with three lines of different lengths. We had to decide which line on the second card was the same length as the line on the first card. The correct answer was easy to pick. The first couple of times when the experimenter requested the answer, we were all correct, but on the next twelve tasks, the accomplices picked a line on the second card that was obviously the wrong answer. I did not give in straight away, but eventually conformed to the group's incorrect decisions.

The experimenters had to debrief me, and during the discussion following my participation, they gave me a copy of Asch's study, and told me a bit about the course.

I was excited about the whole episode. Perhaps I was clever enough after all, to become a psychologist, so the next year, 1976, I tentatively prodded at my dream. I abandoned the English-History major and enrolled in the after-hours first year psychology subject. I topped the class at the end of the year and was offered a place in second year psychology in the science department.

Because psychology at Monash was 'experimental psychology' we had to undertake laboratory work. My first session in the lab. with the late Dr. Stella Crossley left me glassy eyed. It was a genetics class, in which we had to replicate something of Thomas Hunt Morgan's experiments showing chromosomes as the basis for inheritance, first undertaken 70 years before. We had to observe the reproduction of generations of the workhorse of genetic studies, *Drosophila melanogaster* — fruit flies — through a binocular microscope.

D. melanogaster is still used for studying how DNA affects development, because of its simple genetic architecture and the speed with which it can be bred.

A crisis occurred in 2011 in the genetics community, when the body that governs the official naming of animals ruled that D. melanogaster, which means 'dark-bellied dew-lover', be renamed Sophophora melanogaster, meaning 'dark-bellied bearer of wisdom', since recent research shows it to be of a different genus. I have no idea of the eventual outcome of this catastrophe.

Another challenge I had to face in transferring to a science degree was the requirement to learn statistics. I left my first statistics lecture shaking and in tears. I hadn't understood a word of it, and I failed my first statistics test. I became a familiar figure in the Monash library.

'Do you have any easy statistics books?' I would ask. I'd borrow whatever they produced and return it the next day when I couldn't understand it. I finally found an introductory book — for primary school students — in a school bookshop, and understood it. Once I got the basics I managed, and finally gained a high distinction for statistics in my third year. This was an accomplishment for someone who did not know her tables in grade 6, and secretly used her fingers to add up.

I still appreciate the four years of half-time study leave the Victorian Education Department awarded me to undertake an honours degree in psychology. I completed it in 1980, and gained first class honours. I probably could have completed a Doctor of Philosophy at Massachusetts Institute of Technology, but it was out of the question. I had to fulfill a debt of three years full-time work to the Education Department, and my daughters were teenagers. Teresa and Belinda were still at school and did not want to go anywhere, and I was beginning to worry about Vicki.

CHAPTER 6

...AND A LOSS ALONG THE WAY

My eldest daughter Vicki and I shrieked with laughter. 'Look at this one,' she said. She could hardly speak through the laughter.

'*The possems grunt evry night on my roof on there way home to bed in there trees.*'

It was early in 1993. We were sorting out boxes from her childhood that had stayed in her wardrobe after she grew up. I undertook this sorting exercise with each of my three daughters and their wardrobes, when I decided to sell the family home of empty bedrooms, an unused swimming pool, a rusting trampoline and other evidence of a growing family. As each of the three girls had moved out, moved back, travelled overseas, moved back again, sometimes with boyfriends, the detritus of their childhood years continued to lurk in their wardrobes.

Vicki was already suffering symptoms of the serious mental health problems that would eventually overwhelm her, but we had no thought for such matters as we laughed until tears poured from our eyes. In one of the boxes, we had discovered a stash of Vicki's primary school compositions. She had always loved to write, and produced some amazing stories throughout her school years. However, she was of the generation when educational philosophy decreed that concentration on such a mundane task as spelling quelled the creative spirit. Children were encouraged to engage in free writing, and no one seemed to care how they spelled it. The combination of wonderful stories and atrocious spelling had set us both off. We read all her stories and laughed for a couple of hours. I don't know what happened to those stories, but I wish I still had them.

This is the last time I can recall experiencing such pleasure with Vicki. There had been many previous occasions — she had a great sense of humour, but the grey shroud of her mental illness gradually diminished her ability to experience pleasure and joy. It also prevented her family and friends from engaging in honest, loving relationships with her.

Vicki 1973 — before her father's death

Towards the end of 1993, Vicki came to visit me.

'Don't call me Vicki anymore,' she said. 'I've changed my name to Victoria — it has dignity, not like Vicki. Why would you call me such a trivial name anyhow?'

She probably had a point.

'Sorry Vicki, ah, Victoria, I'd just turned 23 and thought it was a lovely name.'

Her name change seemed like an announcement of the accelerating personality change that sent her — and the rest of her family — on a roller coaster ride of mental illness.

❖

When did it start? Why? Was it my fault? Was it her father's death? Was it genetic? I didn't know.

I recalled an incident that seemed strange at the time. It took place when Vicki was in year ten — fifteen or sixteen years old, in 1976. I wondered later if it was early evidence of her developing illness. There had been career talk at school and home. Vicki had an after-school job a couple of days a week at a local music shop, which she loved. She came home from school one day with a plan.

'I'm going to be a professional actor.'

'That's good,' I said, casually, probably not giving her my full attention. 'You might be able to learn acting. P'raps you could go to NIDA.'

'No,' she said. 'I need to join this theatre company now.'

She had a brochure for an amateur theatre company at Clayton, albeit well regarded, forty-five minutes each way by car from home.

'It's twice a week, and I start tomorrow at five o'clock. You have to take me.'

'I can't possibly do that,' I told her. 'I can't come home from school, take you to Clayton, then go my lecture, and I can't take you other nights.

'You're just selfish.'

Guilt tugged at me.

It's at tea time, and it'd take far too long. Join one of the local theatre companies. They're very professional, and I can take you to one of them.'

'No,' she said. 'I have to go to this one.'

'No,' I said.

She threw a tantrum that I still remember vividly, with horror. It was a sixteen-year-old version of one of those three-year-old tantrums common in supermarkets. She saw me as the devil incarnate — I was completely bad. Her extreme behaviour continued for some weeks, and she hung on to my refusal to take her to this theatre company for years, blaming me during the times she perceived me as evil, for preventing her from becoming an actor.

❖

It may be that Peter's sudden death five days before she turned thirteen were triggers that led to the illness that destroyed Vicki. My neglect of her emotional needs following his death may also have been a factor. She always had a 'short fuse', like her father. He was a good and loving husband and father, but his temper would sometimes flair for inexplicable reasons over trivial matters. His early death threw me, and the children, into chaos and Vicki was, in truth, abandoned during the next few months, as I tried to sort out our lives. The two younger girls spent a lot of this time at my mother's place They even attended a primary school near her house for a short time, but Vicki, in year seven at high school, stayed with her best friend's family most of the time in the early weeks, so as not to miss school. She missed out on close family support during that period.

When I look back, I am horrified that I did not allow my daughters, particularly Vicki, just turned thirteen, to attend their father's funeral. They didn't even have that closure. I remember not wanting the children to attend the funeral because I thought it would be too painful for them. Painful or not, the ritual of a funeral can be emotionally healthy. Their father just disappeared, and I was not around much for some months.

❖

As she grew up Vicki didn't show many signs of the illness simmering somewhere within her. She did well at school, had girlfriends, and in year 12, a boyfriend, Kevin, who was in her class. She passed her final exams in year 12, not spectacularly, but solidly. Her marks weren't high enough for Monash University, her first choice. She was devastated at first, but eventually accepted an offer for a Business Studies degree at Swinburne. She decided to defer for a year and join Kevin on a trip overseas. Kevin's family was from England, and he had relatives there with whom they could stay. Vicki had only one relative overseas, her half brother, Michael.

I was dubious about her going overseas so young, with a boyfriend. I already had wisps of concern about aspects of her behaviour and her fluctuating emotions, but couldn't articulate them. But when Vicki wanted something, she could be tenacious. As soon as school finished in 1979, she got a full-time job in the local pickle factory. She worked even more than full-time, doing extra shifts. Summer was pickle-making time as the tomatoes ripened. Over those few months, Teresa and Belinda noticed that the back half of the house smelt constantly of pickles as Vicki carried the aroma with her at all times. The whole family, including Vicki, laughed about it.

Vicki 1979

To her credit, she saved a great deal of money toward her trip, not enough to keep her for the eight months she intended staying — the amount of time Kevin was booked for, but enough for her return fare and plenty to live on for a month or two. My mother and I added some extra funds to her savings, and both Vicki and Kevin insisted there would be no problems getting jobs. She applied for and received a six-month working visa, and bought a return ticket, for eight months. Her flight was due to leave a week earlier that Kevin's, and this troubled me. She said that was the only ticket she could get, but I wondered whether her leaving early was deliberate. She told me she had arranged to stay with her half brother, Michael and his friend, in London, for the week before Kevin arrived. Michael was a drummer in a band in London, and I had been unaware that Vicki was in touch with him. I would have preferred had she not been. I never found out what happened during that week.

❖

Three o'clock in the morning. I was sound asleep until the sound of the phone threw me into nervous wakefulness. A ringing phone in the middle of the night haunted me for the eight months Vicki was away. This first call was dramatic. It came at the end of Vicki's first week in London.

'Mum, Kevin's arrived, and we've broken up.' She was sobbing.

I found out later that Vicki had called the relationship off.

Vicki's regular calls were usually in the middle of my Melbourne night, and often prefaced with long sobs.

'Mum, I've run out of money. Can you send me some?'

'Mum, I've got a job in a shoe factory in Norwich.'

'Mum, I have to come home. I haven't got anywhere to stay, and I haven't got any money.'

'Mum, it's alright; I'm going to Kevin's aunt's place.'

'Mum, I have to come home. You have to buy me a ticket. I can't stand it here any longer.'

I would lie awake for the rest of the night, feeling worried and helpless—no mobiles, e-mail, face-book or twitter in those days, to provide instant relief from a parent's concerns.

❖

Vicki seemed different as she walked across the tarmac eight months after I had last seen her. She had adopted a strong, rather upper class English accent, which took a few months to fade, and she was strange in ways I could not pin down.

She moved back home and showed her usual level of enterprise as she was rehired at the music shop and started business studies at Swinburne Institute, a train trip to Hawthorn. She excelled academically and at her job, filling in as manager in the latter when the owner was away. On the surface, she seemed a reasonable happy young woman, but flickers of emotional cracks flared occasionally. They seemed to impede her progression into adulthood. She seemed not to be able to see the world from others' points of view, and to have little insight into the effect of her own behaviour on others, like a two year old.

This aspect of maturity has since been labelled 'emotional intelligence' and is seen as more important in the workplace than general intelligence measured by intelligence quotient (IQ) tests.

Vicki had a high IQ, but she started having trouble with friendships at university, difficulty with working in groups, and volatile, short-lived relationships. At home, regular temper tantrums caused the rest of us distress. I still remember one occasion. Teresa, then about seventeen, had some friends over. Vicki had gone to bed early, and at about half past eight, she stormed out of her room, red faced, screaming with rage.

'Be quiet. I can't sleep. You're too noisy.'

Teresa's friends went home, and Teresa felt humiliated. Vicki went back to bed, but the next day, as usually happened, had forgotten her outburst.

Vicki still had a delightful sense of humour, and could still send the rest of the family into paroxysms of laughter, once everyone had recovered from her last outburst of rage. She entertained us with wonderful imitations of teachers at Bayswater High School, the school that the three girls had attended. She would compose hilarious plays and organise her sisters into parts, which they would perform for me with much laughter all round.

She topped her year on completion of her degree, and was offered a graduate position with Telstra, where she stayed for almost ten years, gaining regular promotions. She lived at home while she studied at Swinburne, and came and went between periods in share houses until she married. She had boyfriends, who were invariably 'lovely young men', as my mother and I would say to each other. However, the relationships never lasted. Vicki would have tantrums and end the relationships.

She still yearned to be a famous actor or singer, and in 1985 advertised in a newspaper for a guitar-playing accompanist for her singing. Jeff Hackett, who later became Vicki's husband, responded to the advertisement, and they had great fun strumming and singing in our lounge room or, in their words, 'rehearsing for our first gig.' Jeff had studied engineering, and had completed a degree, but was living an 'alternative' lifestyle, that is, he wasn't working. However, like most of the men with whom Vicki became involved, he was a gentle person, with an easygoing nature.

They became engaged in late 1985, with their marriage to take place sometime in the unnamed future. I remember organising a successful engagement party at home. Vicki was the happiest she had been since before her trip overseas seven years before.

❖

Meanwhile another tragedy loomed. At the age of 74, my mother, Dorothy Murphy, was extremely fit, despite the rheumatoid arthritis she had developed three months after my brother's death in 1966. She also suffered from osteoporosis, but regular walking kept her in good shape. She spent a lot of time at our place, regularly walking the two kilometres to and from her unit.

Early in 1982, she fell and broke her hip. I did not realise what was wrong and instead of calling an ambulance, I drove her to the Austin Hospital. I still experience twinges of guilt about this, because she moaned in pain at every jerk of the car. She had a hip replacement operation, but it was not successful. Within a few months of the operation, the bone around the hip replacement gave way and the prosthesis collapsed. She had a second operation, which enabled her to walk reasonably well, although one leg was a little shorter than the other was, causing her to limp.

Three years after she broke her hip, she was diagnosed with lung cancer, despite being a non-smoker. However, she'd lived with my father, a chain-smoker, for 35 years. I imagine the passive smoke she inhaled over those years caused the cancer.

❖

My mother died on 31 March 1986. After her funeral service, before we headed to the New Cheltenham cemetery for her burial, Vicki announced to me, Teresa and Teresa's then boyfriend, Brendan, that she had an appointment in five minutes with a local doctor for a check-up, to do with her pregnancy,.

'You have to take me,' she said to me. 'I told you I'm 16 weeks pregnant.'

She hadn't — and it turned out that she was about ten weeks pregnant. I reminded her we were in the middle of her grandmother's funeral, which took precedence, so she threw a massive tantrum — screamed that I did not care about her. I left for the New Cheltenham Cemetery, and Teresa and Brendan organised Vicki. I am still grateful to them for that.

❖

Vicki was a paradox, where two sides of her personality seemed to be warring for supremacy. Sadly, her wonderful qualities were gradually submerged by those that eventually destroyed her.

CHAPTER 7

HOUSEWIFE, PSYCHOLOGIST, POLITICIAN

Meanwhile the rest of my life continued its transition from housewife to psychologist to parliamentarian. I'd only had a three year half-time study award, and I needed a fourth. I found the person with the power and applied for another year to complete my honours year.

'No,' came the unqualified reply.

So I rang or wrote every week, requesting a change of mind. I bombarded the poor bureaucrat with evidence of my work, letters of recommendation and pleas.

Just before the closing date for honours applicants, he relented.

'Only one year,' the letter stated sternly.

I was elated, even though it meant I had to complete the full-time year in half the time.

I made it — first class honours.

The next year I was promoted from teaching to the Psychology and Guidance Branch of the Education Department. I had to undertake a part-time Education Department training course in educational psychology over two years, while I practised as a psychologist, under supervision, in a group of local primary and secondary schools. I loved my job, which fulfilled my early dream. I became involved in the Victorian Teachers' Union as well and was elected to the Union State Council. I met former Premier John Brumby, who was a union organiser in our area prior to his election the Federal Parliament in 1983. It was partly through this association that my professions as psychologist and parliamentarian first crossed paths.

I had joined the Labor Party early in the 1970s. In those days, I attended local branch meetings and helped in election campaigns. I was too nervous to say much and made the tea at the end of the meeting. As the 1970s rolled along, attitudes towards women in the Union movement and the Labor Party changed — reluctantly — to mirror society generally. I changed too, as I gained confidence.

During the 1974 campaign that elected the Whitlam government for the second time, my involvement went beyond handing out 'how-to-vote' cards on election day. I spent weekends 'door-knocking' in street after street in the electorate of Casey, where I lived, and where Race Mathews, who'd been elected in 1972, was standing again.

I'd speak to women who seemed pleased to talk to me.

'We need to re-elect the Whitlam government,' I'd suggest, as I'd remind them of the progressive policies of the Whitlam Government that particularly benefitted women. I thoroughly enjoyed the task. I helped with campaigns on and off through the seventies, although I became disillusioned for a while and let my membership lapse for a time. I joined the feminist collective at Monash during that period. However, I joined Labor again, and the Party gradually became part of my extended family.

❖

According to family lore, I was conceived in a tent, where my parents lived for some time during the depression of the 1930s. My father, along with hundreds of others, was employed on a government project digging irrigation channels in the Mallee in northern Victoria. Tents were provided for workers so that it was easy to move from job to job — basic accommodation, but at least my parents were sheltered from the weather, and had enough to eat.

Once my mother became pregnant, they had to move from the Mallee, since she suffered from *pernicious vomiting*, and needed to attend the Queen Victoria hospital in Melbourne. In early 1937, jobs for unskilled workers like my father were hard to come by in Melbourne, so they moved in with my Grandma in Windsor. I remember Grandma's house as my first home. I grew up hearing stories of my parents' hardship during the depression, so when I discovered the challenge of social policy development during the 1970s, these stories may have contributed to the strong interest in housing I developed during the 1970s and early 1980s.

As well, I learned in psychology about Abraham Maslow's ubiquitous theory of human needs, which proposes a hierarchy with each level built on previous ones. The first level of needs includes basics such as food, water, shelter and safety. If people cannot satisfy these needs, they can achieve no more in life. They are stuck. Maslow's theory makes sense.

I decided that affordable housing was a right that should be available to all, even to the poorest people in society. I joined the Labor Party's Housing Policy Committee, and in the early 1980s when home loan interest rates, including mine, were increasing dramatically, instigated a lobby group, *The Home Interest Association*. Its purpose was to persuade the Federal Government — Malcolm Fraser's Liberal Government that had stolen government from Gough Whitlam in 1975 — to keep housing interest rates at an affordable level. This was before the 1983 deregulation of the financial system by Paul Keating, Treasurer in the Hawke Government

Another driver of my interest in housing was a belief in an egalitarian society — that I still hold, theoretically — which would require affordable housing and redistribution of land.

An early conflict about land ownership took place in Victoria in the latter part of the 19th century, when squatters had claimed ownership of most of the good land throughout rural Victoria. The government was under strong pressure to make land available for the broader population. Squatters and the Legislative Council fought these pressures, but eventually the government freed small blocks of land for selection by people aspiring to farm.

Both sets of my grandparents were among those who selected land in the Mallee. They grew wheat and ran dairy cattle, but since both sets of my grandparents produced eight children, there was not enough to land to share with all family members. The only option available for poor families was to rent or live with other family members.

❖

Victoria's first attempt to provide low-cost housing in Melbourne on a single estate was the Garden City project, commenced in 1926 through the State Savings Bank of Victoria. The bank hired architects Henderson and Haddow to build more than 300 houses. The nature of this project influenced the design of the large public housing estates developed later by the Housing Commission of Victoria.

The theory behind the design is fascinating. There were conflicting needs to use as little land as possible, while still allowing outdoor play areas to encourage healthy development of children. In Garden City the units were all double story 'pairs', with room for gardens around three sides of each house.

The Housing Commission of Victoria was established in March 1938, following an investigation by a Parliamentary Committee into the nature of workers' housing in the inner suburbs — where most job opportunities for blue-collar workers were situated — and a campaign by social reformer Oswald Barnett. The committee expressed shock at the poor living conditions of many working families.

Atherton Street Fitzroy, late 1950s.
Source: JL O'Brien Collection, University of Melbourne Archives

The Housing Commission's brief was twofold — to provide as much low-cost housing of reasonable quality for working families as they could, and to undertake slum clearance. The theory of using as little land as possible for low cost housing, while providing children's play areas still held, so slums were torn down and replaced with 21 blocks of high-rise Housing Commission flats that are spread through inner Melbourne suburbs. The part of the theory that said, 'use less land' won over 'children need space'. A large area of open space was provided around each high-rise block of flats, but it didn't occur to the men who developed the policies that it was not safe for children to use the open space without supervision. No one had asked women what they wanted.

Aerial view of Collingwood showing high-rise Housing Commission flats

Source: Wikipedia

❖

By the early 1940s my father had a steady job, first as a storeman, and later, after he studied, as a bookkeeper with Malcolm Moore Industries, one of Australia's largest engineering companies. My parents became part of the lucky 50 percent of Australians who were buying or owned a house. It was in suburban Hawthorn with the deposit provided by my mother's family. I remember flowery carpet on the floor, a lavatory near the back door that flushed when you pulled a chain, a soft green velvet lawn and sweet peas climbing a fence. My mother was the happiest she had ever been, with secure, comfortable shelter near her extended family.

Over the next 30 years, rates of home ownership grew from 50 percent to 70 percent of Australian families, due to government subsidies that helped provide affordable loans to people to buy their own homes.

My husband and I built our first new home in Bayswater with finance from a government subsidised cooperative housing loan — it was called something like, 'Ringwood cooperative Housing Society number 42,' meaning that we were the 42nd group of home builders to gain finance from this group of co-operative housing societies.

❖

I became a candidate in the historic 1982 Victorian election by default. The Secretary of the local Branch of the Labor Party begged me to stand for electorate of Wantirna, since they couldn't find a candidate. I didn't win, but gained a respectable swing and missed out by 0.3 percent.

'You didn't lose, just failed to win.' My colleagues grinned.

I went back to my job as a psychologist, still loved it but I had the politics bug as well. The electorate of Wantirna was poised for a Labor Party win at the next election.

No one begged me to stand for Wantirna at the 1985 election, and I didn't wait to be asked.

'I intend to stand for the election.' I'd learned that self promotion and an assertive attitude are useful attributes for an aspiring politician.

It was classified as a definite Labor win, and plenty of potential candidates, more eminent in the Party than I was, were eying it off. Friends had advised me that if I wanted a look-in for the 1985 election I would need support from a faction. I had to decide which faction, and join. I found the choice easy. My philosophy fitted the Left faction, and some local Party members I respected were in the Left, so I joined.

Once nominations opened for selection of a Labor candidate, I appreciated the support of the Left. My opponent, Dick Coughlin, was a protégée of Steve Crabb, Member for the next-door electorate of Knox, Minister for Transport and a member of the Right faction.

I thought I'd developed confidence, but this preselection taught me I had a long way to go. I was almost overwhelmed with anxiety throughout the process. I was not a 'natural' at politics. My personality and background had imbued me with a high need for approval, and although the 'battle' of letters and phone calls leading up to voting day was not meant to be personal, it felt as though it was. I managed to hide my feelings publicly — necessary in politics. I remember friends telling me about receiving phone calls from the late Pauline Toner, to women Labor Party members, recommending they vote for Dick Coughlin. There was also a letter signed by Premier John Cain, supporting my opponent, understandably, since Dick worked as a Ministerial Adviser, and was a more attractive asset to Government than I was.

The preselection was held in the Council Chamber at the Trades Hall. I don't remember much about it, except that I learned my five-minute speech off by heart, and was nearly sick with fear as I stood on the podium. I won the preselection, not because my speech was persuasive, but because my faction, the Left, held a majority of votes on the preselection panel and members had been instructed to vote for me.

❖

By the late 1970s Cooperative Housing Societies had virtually disappeared, and most homebuyers were under the thumb of the major banks. Suddenly, everyone's home loan interest rates, including mine, began to increase, leading to increases in mortgage repayments.

A small group of friends and I decided to do something about it. We organised a public meeting to discuss and protest against rising interest rates. I publicised the meeting widely through the media, who were all happy to oblige with interviews, and on the night of the meeting we were astonished to see the Bayswater Community Hall (now the Knox Arts Centre) filled to capacity. Peter Couchman, then an ABC Current Affairs journalist, arrived with a film crew to cover the meeting and it ran on television.

I had never spoken publicly from a stage before, never used a microphone, and I can still remember shaking so much as I stood on the stage at the start of the meeting that I could hardly get the words out. However, it was a great success, and at the end, almost all attendees left their contact details, paid a 50 cent fee, and gave birth to the Home Interest Association of Victoria, which became an effective lobby group, giving voice to the concerns of homebuyers with increasing mortgages.

The organisation and its membership came and went for a decade, depending on whether interest rates were rising or falling. A small core group kept going, and used the once off payment of the 50 cent membership fee to publish and distribute occasional newsletters, and organise irregular meetings. At its lowest point, my friend Heather O'Connor suggested that she, my mother and I were the only members, while at other times, when interest rates rose, hundreds of people would join or rejoin.

The Home Interest Association lost much of its lobbying power in 1983 after newly elected Labor Federal Treasurer Paul Keating implemented most recommendations of the seminal *Committee of Inquiry into the Australian Financial System,* chaired by Sir Keith Campbell. Australia's financial system changed dramatically with the implementation of the report, as the dollar was floated, interest rates were deregulated and their control was passed from the government to the Reserve Bank of Australia.

As a member of the Labor Party Housing Policy Committee, I joined in the work of developing policy that would expand the marginalised public housing sector into a viable rental option for the general community, as happens in Holland and other European countries. It never happened, although the policies of moving public housing from inner city 'ghettos' to a spread in suburban streets are still in place. The government introduced the first public housing in the Eastern suburbs and built public housing to the same standard as private sector housing, so the two tenures would be indistinguishable. It also poured large amounts of money into refurbishing the high rise flats surrounding inner Melbourne.

However, rapid expansion of the sector was stymied when

the Commonwealth government, from whom most funds came to Victoria, through the Commonwealth-State Housing agreement, changed its priorities. Instead of direct funding for the provision of public housing, funds were to go straight to tenants in the private rental sector as rent assistance. Public housing, or social housing, is still marginalised, giving priority to people with special needs and has a years-long waiting list for low income earners.

During the late 1980s, while I still had stars of idealism in my eyes, I managed to persuade the Minister of the day to listen to women's views about housing. He established a Ministerial Advisory Committee on Women and Housing, and invited me to chair it. It was an exciting time, as the members were a vibrant, talented group. We auspiced a consultation of Victorian women to find out what they thought was important for housing.

I reproduce excerpts from my foreword to the report, *Speaking of Housing,* below.

> ...*Women have traditionally had little involvement at any level in the provision of housing in Victoria, either in the public or private sectors. There have been few women involved in planning and urban design, which decides the location of housing, its density, surrounding environment and accompanying services.*

> ...*At the same time women have traditionally been termed 'home-makers' whose role is crucial in 'turning a house into a home'...*

❖

In recent years, housing costs have spiralled again, this time not due to interest rate rises, but to increased house and land prices and the size of mortgages and rents. Social commentators are discussing the need for affordable shelter once more as it has emerged as an important social issue.

An *Age* article by Michael Pascoe (Oct 11 2011) about the tax forum in Canberra pointed out the tax-based problems with housing affordability, which politicians are afraid to confront. He ventured to suggest that public housing might be a better economic proposition than subsided private housing. Hooray. Here are some excerpts.

> *...[Housing affordability] was a major issue in the state taxation discussion, it flared as a social welfare issue during the transfers session, the negative gearing aspects were there in personal taxation, there were housing affordability ramifications in the observation that we have a tax system that favours those who borrow and speculate over those who work and save.*
>
> *And this was just taxation - only part of the housing affordability problem...*
>
> *...Last week I watched all nine federal, state and territory treasurers either explicitly or implicitly acknowledge that they're running taxation policies that are bad for the nation because of their impact on housing, perverting the more efficient use of land, worsening affordability, making poverty worse...*
>
> *...The Henry taxation review team primarily liked the idea of a broad land tax because it was efficient - land can't up and run away to a tax haven and it's rather hard to disguise - but it also has important positive aspects.*

For a start, it would replace bad state transaction taxes that inhibit mobility, that are disincentives on boomers downsizing and workers moving to where the work is...

...Then there's negative gearing as we presently know it, a subject aired often enough for everyone to have their vested interests confirmed...

...There's an efficiency question to be worked through on whether it makes sense for taxpayers to subsidise demand for privately owned accommodation, or to build more public social housing, given the much cheaper borrowing costs for government...

Perhaps Governments should take note of the economics of directly funding housing. It should remove negative gearing, broaden the land tax base and remove rent subsidies, and pour the money saved into direct provision of rental housing in competition with private landlords. That will be the day!

❖

I hoped when I was elected to Parliament I would be able to make a real difference to people's lives by ensuring that they would be able to fulfill their ambitions, from the security and safety of a home they could afford to live in.

CHAPTER 8
'MAIDEN' SPEECH

'**D**id you get those medals for killing people?'

My daughter questioned Sir Brian Murray, former Naval Admiral and the Governor of Victoria. My family was with me at the party in the Victorian Parliamentary gardens following the opening of the fiftieth Parliament of Victoria, on Monday April 3rd 1985.

The deciduous trees were shrugging into their autumn tweed coats, but the detritus of their spring and summer profusion had been raked and hidden, leaving the lawns perfectly styled. A white canvas marquee ballooned on the broad sweep of green. Food, drinks and chatter were based there, while groups wove around the gravel paths that were to become so familiar to me over the years.

It was an exciting day for my mother, my three daughters and me. For me, because I had just been sworn in as the Member for Wantirna in the Legislative Assembly, and had participated in the ritual of the opening of a new Parliament. My family was thrilled for me, and enjoyed the day thoroughly — none of them had ever been inside the historic Victorian Parliament House and gardens before.

I did not give my daughter a chance to hear any response the Governor may have offered. I dragged her away.

'He's the Governor,' I said. 'Don't be impertinent.'

❖

John Cain became Premier of Victoria in 1982, following his father's earlier footsteps. This was the first Labor Government since John Cain senior lost government in 1955. Then, a group of Labor Members of Parliament crossed the floor on a Bill and defected to the Democratic Labor Party (DLP). The reason for the twenty-seven year gap between the governments of father and son was the DLP allocation of preferences to the Liberal Party throughout those years.

There is an adage that oppositions do not win elections, governments lose them. However, on this occasion the demise of the DLP and a talented Parliamentary Labor Party contributed to the Cain Government's comfortable 1982 win.

John Cain with his well-prepared team of Ministers, who knew their portfolio areas, began an ambitious program of legislation to implement policies taken to the election, and to convert the Victorian Statute book to plain English. Some Acts had remained untouched for up to 130 years. In its first term, the Labor Government passed 448 pieces of legislation, including the landmark Equal Opportunity Act in 1984. This Act dramatically enhanced the participation of women in the workforce and in society generally.

After the election, held on 5 March, 1985, I felt pleased with myself. *The people have chosen me.* A ponderous thought, particularly since my win was to do with the popularity of the Cain Government rather than through my efforts.

The first meeting of Caucus (the Parliamentary Labor Party) brought me back to politics in the raw. The welcome to our cohort of new Members was minimal, as there was a standoff between the factions and the Premier over who should serve in Cabinet. Instead of a negotiated outcome, each faction *and* the Premier produced 'how to vote' tickets. The voting system required repeated ballots until all but the required number of candidates were eliminated. There was little discussion.

'The result of this ballot is …'

''… is eliminated. Next ballot.'

'The result of this ballot is …'

The main speaker was the returning officer.

Voting went on for hours in an unfriendly atmosphere. The little conversation that involved me was someone from the Left ensuring I had filled in my ballot paper correctly.

'Show me your ballot paper, Carolyn,' again and again.

The process meant little to those of us who were newly elected, and we were relieved when the Caucus meeting was finally over.

❖

What a privilege. I was to move that the Legislative Assembly agree to the Governor's speech outlining the policies and plans of the new Government, delivered earlier in the day. Newly elected Members of Parliament usually make the first speeches of this 'Address in Reply'. Over the next weeks, most Members contributed to the debate, describing how the Government's policies would apply to their electorates.

I'd laboured for days writing this speech, and stood in my allotted place in the back row with sweating hands, thumping heart and a dry mouth. I was allowed to read it, and was not interrupted, a courtesy offered to Members for their 'maiden' speeches. My voice shook as I started, but I settled in after a minute or two. The term 'maiden speech' referring to inaugural speeches is a custom from the British Parliament — ironic in the old all male establishment.

These excerpts of my 'maiden' speech taken from Hansard — the Parliamentary record — don't shake or sweat. They sit calmly on the page, providing no clues to the manner of their delivery.

Mrs HIRSH (Wantirna)—I move:

That the following Address-in-Reply to the Speech of His Excellency the Governor to both Houses of Parliament be agreed to by this House—

YOUR EXCELLENCY:

We, the Legislative Assembly of Victoria, assembled in Parliament, wish to express our loyalty to our Sovereign, and to thank your Excellency for the Speech which you have made to the Parliament.

I am honoured to move the motion for the adoption of the Address-in-Reply. This task is of great significance because of the special circumstances surrounding today's opening of Parliament. This is the fiftieth Parliament in this State and it is meeting in the year of Victoria's 150th anniversary. It is an historic occasion, in that a Labor Government has been re-elected for a second term by the people of Victoria. That has never happened in this State before. Also, it is exactly three years today since the election of the first Cain Labor Government of this generation...

...As one of the eight women on the Government side of the House, I direct attention to the fact that it is 61 years since women became eligible to stand as candidates at Parliamentary elections in this State. The electorate of Wantirna is unique in Victoria, in that it is now wholly represented by women. When I look around the Chamber, it is obvious to me that the Labor Party is the only party that has taken steps to ensure that women are being represented in Parliament...

...With the historic election of this Government, history has also been made in the electorate of Wantirna. For the first time, a member of the Labor Party has been elected to represent the people of Wantirna. I am honoured to represent the electorate in this Parliament and I thank the people of Wantirna for so clearly placing their confidence in me at the recent poll...

...I should explain how I came to be in this place. I have chosen to pursue a political career because I believe Government intervention in the affairs of society is essential

*for the purposes of alleviating poverty and ensuring that
there is an equitable distribution of available resources to
all people. I worked for many years as a teacher and as a
psychologist with individuals and families who are considered
to be disadvantaged. I have reached the conclusion that, for
a majority of disadvantaged people, the main difficulties
they face are a lack of availability of resources or a lack of
accessibility to the resources that exist. I refer to such matters
as economic resources, through jobs and income support,
housing, transport, education, child care and health care.
People have a right to these resources and Governments have
a responsibility to provide them...*

*...Finally, I wish to mention the right of people to live their
lives in safety. The Victorian Labor Government's policy of a
nuclear-free State provides a model for Australia and for the
rest of the world in bringing about disarmament and bans on
all nuclear weapons. I shall encourage the declaration of the
City of Knox as a nuclear-free zone as part of this program.*

*I look forward to energetically and effectively representing in
Parliament the electorate of Wantirna during the second Cain
Labor Government of the 1980s.*

The sitting was suspended at 6.25 p.m. until 8.04.

❖

At exactly eight o'clock, the bells rang to summon members
back to work. They sounded from every office and every nook

and cranny of the Parliament — two lots of bells, red and green. Red for the Legislative Council and green for the 'peoples' house', the Legislative Assembly. How can bells be coloured? They sounded the same. You had to look at them to see which colour they were. After a meal break, they rang until there was a quorum, and for three minutes when members were summoned for a vote if a division was called.

My inaugural speech over, I had a chance to relax a little and allow the atmosphere of the Chamber to seep through my senses — and examine this illustrious workplace I would be a part of for at least the next three years. The room itself is windowless — there were windows once I believe — and the décor is relatively plain, at least relative to the Legislative Council Chamber.

Both Chambers were built in 1856, rectangular buildings, the same size on the outside. In 1985, Members sat on three rows of green leather benches, lining three sides of the Chamber. The Government always occupies those to the right of the Speaker, the Opposition the left, and the National Party and 'oddments', for whom there is no room on the side benches, are allocated seats along the back, facing the Speaker. The seating design then supported an adversarial system, as Government and Opposition faced each other across the table in the centre of the room, and threw verbal barbs, rocks and spears at one another. As a new member, I was assigned a seat along the back row.

Experienced Members advised me to spend time in the Chamber, watching, listening and learning. My first contribution, two weeks after my inaugural speech, was a 'Dorothy Dix' question without notice to the Minister for Public Works, 'Bunna' Walsh, asking for a report on the progress of the new TAFE College under construction in Wantirna. I can remember my wet hands and dry mouth again as I waited to leap to my feet.

'If you don't get up quickly, you'll miss your turn, and the question will go to the Opposition,' the Whip instructed me as he handed me my typed question.

The adjournment debate, another fortnight later, was my next speaking venture, still shaking, heart thumping, sweaty hands. I had five minutes to speak, and used it to point out the intersections in my electorate that required traffic lights — somewhat short of my policy goals to bring about housing affordability and a just society.

In the Spring Session, in October 1985, I spoke on a Bill to ratify the Commonwealth–State Housing agreement. As soon as I started to speak, Jeff Kennett, then Leader of the Opposition, interjected. This was to become a pattern for the rest of my first term. But the Bill was not controversial, and I managed to get through the ten minutes or so on my feet reasonably well. This led me to become overconfident.

My next speech, a few weeks later, on a Bill to increase the rights of tenants in private rental housing, was a disaster. I felt quite proud to be first speaker for the Government in the second reading debate, but realised later it was because no-one else wanted to speak on it. A controversial Bill, it ended up drastically amended in the Legislative Council before becoming law.

I had made a speech explaining the legislation to a hall full of hostile — but polite — real estate agents and landlords the previous evening, and decided to repeat the speech in the House the next day.

Two sentences in, Jeff Kennett interjected, calling out, 'Socialisation!' The rest of the time I was on my feet my words were punctuated with shouted interjections and 'points of order' from Opposition Members.

I sat down eventually, in tears, and learned some important lessons from the experience. Speaking in an adversarial House of Parliament is difficult, particularly on a controversial matter. It requires more practice than I had, and I was still living with the illusion that I could bring about an ideal world with progressive legislation.

The speaker following me in the debate, a liberal, John Richardson, the member for Forest Hill, made the point about reality versus idealism.

'The bill is the ultimate triumph of ideology over commonsense and the triumph of rhetoric over reality. Nowhere is that more evident than in the remarks of the honourable member for Wantirna. I do not doubt the honourable member's zeal but I doubt her common sense, her capacity to distinguish ideology from reality...'

I recovered from the mortification of that speech. However, when I reread it in Hansard twenty-five years later, I felt a hot flush of embarrassment again, and the discomfort of the cushions on the old green leather bench at the back of the Chamber. I saw the small black microphone that propelled my words to every office in the Parliament, and the Hansard reporters in the far corner recording my words for posterity.

I went back to watching and learning for the rest of the session, and began to understand why Margaret Ray and Jane Hill, two of the dedicated 'pioneer' women elected in 1982, were reluctant to speak in the House.

My next speech, ironically, was about alcohol, particularly about teenage and underage drinking. A new beverage, called

Cooler, had recently been introduced into the Australian market. It was the first of the sweetened wine or spirit based alcoholic drinks that taste like soft drink, and are now ubiquitous. Time has shown that I was correct in pointing out their danger for young people, but that I was unsuccessful in preventing their proliferation.

❖

By the end of my first term, I had gained some skill at speaking in Parliament, and had learned how to deal with interjections by ignoring them, or replying with a witty quip. None of us — the women — engaged in the childish 'shouting down' that some of the men used to attempt to discomfort a speaker.

A problem for women speakers if they attempted to use vocal colour in a speech, or speak with feeling about an issue, was the tendency of some opposition members to call out,

'Why don't you take a valium?'

The late Gordon Hockley, who sat in a corner near my seat in the back row, told me about bromide.

'When I was in the navy,' he said, 'they'd put bromide in the men's tea, to hose down their libido. Why don't you suggest that to the oppostition next time they shout?'

'You need some bromide in your tea,' was trivial repartee, but it worked. The women heard no more suggestions about valium after that, and my parliamentary performance improved rapidly without the barrage of interjections from the opposition, particularly its leader.

❖

Part of the expected role of a backbench Member of Parliament is to participate in a Parliamentary Committee. I joined the Social Development Committee, chaired by Legislative Council member, Judith Dixon. Committee work was challenging and exciting, with the most interesting inquiry I participated in being the Inquiry into *Options for Dying with Dignity*. The original purpose of the brief from government was to investigate the pros and cons of euthanasia, but was broadened to include intrusive medical treatment, refusal of treatment by patients, recognition of patients' rights should they become incompetent, and palliative care. The committee found at the time, almost twenty-five years ago, that the community was not ready to embrace active euthanasia. The *Medical Treatment Act*, based on the Committee's recommendations, was passed in 1988.

Twenty years later, in 2008, Colleen Hartland, a Member of the Greens in the Legislative Council, and Ken Smith, a Liberal Party Member in the lower house, sponsored a Private Member's Bill to legalise euthanasia — the Medical Treatment (Physician Assisted Dying) Bill, 2008. Colleen Hartland introduced it into the Legislative Council, but it was defeated on the floor of the House. It seems that the community is still not ready for voluntary euthanasia.

I was also involved with developing recommendations for the Psychologists' Registration Bill, which replaced the outdated Psychological Practices Act (1965).

Parliamentary and committee work are only two of the diverse aspects of the role of a Member of Parliament. The job included constituent work in the electorate, which often required my psychological skills, especially if someone rang or came to the office angry or distressed. My staff and I dealt with all sorts of constituent enquiries and problems in the electorate office, grim, tragic, frightening and occasionally hilarious. One unforgettable incident, while potentially serious, made us laugh.

The phones in the electorate office were running hot as usual. Erica put a call through to me.

'I can't deal with this one Carolyn. You look after it,' she said.

A panicked voice came on the line.

'I'm at work in Ringwood and my wife's at home in Wantirna South with our two toddlers. There's a massive tiger snake in the back yard near the door. The children are playing in the sandpit near the back fence. Can you please help? I've just rung the local police station, too.'

I put my constituent on hold and phoned the Council.

'Yes, we have a gang mowing nearby. I'll send them there straight away.'

I got back on the line to my constituent. 'It's sorted out,' I said. 'The Council will be there shortly. They'll deal with the snake.'

The phone rang again. It was the constituent's wife, in a panic.

'Two men from the Council are here,' she said. They passed the children to me, and were about to hit the snake with a shovel, but there's a problem.'

'What?'

'Two policemen have just turned up and told the Council guys they aren't allowed to kill the snake.'

'Put the police on,' I said.

'They're not allowed to kill it Mrs. Hirsh. It's a tiger snake and it's a protected native species,' said the policeman.

'Look,' I said. 'You can't just leave the snake in the back yard. The woman's terrified.'

One of the Council workers came to the phone.

'They'll arrest us if we kill it Mrs. Hirsh. We can't.'

'Can't you do something?' I asked. 'Like take it away?'

'No. the police won't let us near it.'

I rang the Minister for Conservation, Forests and Lands, the department that administered the Wildlife Act that contained the clauses protecting the snake. Joan Kirner, the Minister at the time, came to the phone, chuckling.

'Couldn't leave this one to my advisors,' she said.

She read the relevant sections of the Act to me, leaving me in no doubt that the police officers had interpreted the Act correctly.

'We do have an Official Government Snake Catcher though,' she told me. 'He can get there about 5.30 pm. Sorry it has to be so late. There isn't much call for his services so he only works at snake-catching part-time.'

My constituent rang the next morning to thank me, and reported that the Official Government Snake Catcher had turned up with a couple of sticks and a sack.

'The snake was in the sack, and gone in a couple of minutes,' she said. 'He left me a bill for $50.'

❖

An important part of a Member of Parliament's job was to keep in touch with local organisations and attend functions. These activities occupied most days and many evenings when Parliament was not sitting. I became familiar with residents, businesses and organisations in the Wantirna electorate. Interchange, the multiple birth society, Lutheran Homes for the aged, the Italian Club were a few of the organisations I was involved with during my first Parliamentary term. I loved the job, but felt quite nervous when the Premier announced an election for 1 October 1988.

Speaking at a
community meeting 1986

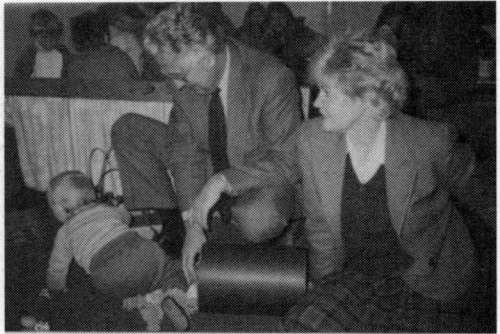

With Minister for Community Services
Race Mathews visiting a Childcare
Centre in Wantirna.

In an immense leap, computers had been installed in electorate offices early that year. The glaring blue monitor with a flickering white dash in the top left corner was both exciting and intimidating. The computer contained a 30 megabyte hard disk drive, and the Steve Jobs miracle of graphic desktops was yet to come. However, we learned to write bulk mail letters to groups in the electorate. Modern campaigning had started.

I sent copies of my speeches to families who lived near upgraded schools, newly duplicated roads, improved train and bus timetables, new traffic lights and anything else, no matter how trivial, that I managed to achieve for *my* people of Wantirna. I wanted to win the next election so much. And I did.

Premier John Cain launching my 1988 election campaign

CHAPTER 9

RE-ELECTED —
PLEASURE AND PAIN

George Seitz rushed into my office, agitated.

'What have I done to deserve this, comrade?'

'Just as you asked George. I assigned you an office on your own,' I said. 'What's the problem?'

'Come and see.'

Room 61A was easy to find. George threw open the door to expose a male urinal.

'You really had it in for me, Hirsh,' he said. 'There isn't even anywhere for me to sit down.'

❖

Election night 1988 was one of the high points of my life. It almost equalled graduating with first class honours in psychology eight years before. *Hopeless Carolyn Murphy from Cressy with the drunken father.* I was so proud to be re-elected to represent Wantirna. *The people like me.*

The Labor Caucus elected me to the position of Government Whip, which came about through machinations between my friend the late Beth Gleeson and me before the election. Beth was elected at the same time as I was in 1985 to Thomastown, the safest seat in Victoria. Like me, she was a member of the Left. Beth worked with dedication for her electorate of Thomastown, especially for the large population of migrant women. She established neighbourhood houses in her electorate, and championed the neighbourhood house movement throughout Victoria. She helped establish the Northern Institute of Technical and Further Education (TAFE), and served on its Council. But she had to watch her back to ensure a number of putative career politicians, searching for a permanent job, did not undermine her, as they looked at her seat with envy. This problem was foreign to marginal seat-holders, since young, ambitious Labor apparatchiks were not interested in marginal seats that changed hands every few elections.

Beth and I decided we did not have enough support to gain Cabinet positions in our second term, so we worked out what positions we could achieve. Beth wanted to chair the Economic Parliamentary Committee. I wanted to be Whip. I still have no idea why. Because we set our sights at realistic levels, we both achieved our goals.

I was a novelty as the first woman in Australia to be elected to the position of Whip. The media, predictably, labelled me Madam Lash, while some of my colleagues called me Mrs. Whippy. My friend and colleague, Margaret Ray, Member for

Box Hill, suggested my job reminded her of picking up the pajamas — an allusion to the traditional role of women at home keeping the house in order.

Election day 1988, with my first granddaughter, Jessica

❖

My first task as Whip was to assign offices in Parliament House to Labor Party Legislative Assembly Members. It was difficult — first, since the Victorian Parliament House was built in bits and pieces from 1856, and second because most of the 'better' offices were carpeted in red, which meant they belonged to the Legislative Council.

Parliament House is a beautiful heritage building, but a warren, with office space hidden along passages and in strange corners. Because Labor was in government, we had a choice of the superior offices, which were not much by 1980s standards. Of course, the Premier, Deputy Premier and Leader of the House had spaces specifically assigned to them, and the Opposition leadership occupied a group of green-carpeted offices in the same passage as the Whip's office.

About forty new offices were available in the 'dungeon' for Ministers and senior backbenchers. Dungeon? Spaces between bluestone buttresses along two corridors had been converted into attractive but windowless offices.

Ministers had offices to themselves, while backbench Members were obliged to share, since there were simply not enough offices to go round. The Whip's job was to work out which Members to put together — sorted by gender, faction and seniority. Most backbench Members were assigned to the 'chook house', a prefabricated portable building in the gardens, officially known as the temporary accommodation. It boasted swaying squeaky floors and green carpeting of course, with small offices opening along a central passage.

I had a map of the Parliament, showing the available spaces, and felt I did a good job placing Members in offices with people they felt comfortable with. George Seitz provided me with my only problem when he informed me that as a senior member of Caucus he should have an office to himself. I perused the map to see whether there was a spare office in any corner. I found one, a small office, number 61A, under a spiral staircase, which I assigned to George. I proudly placed the list of offices in the Labor Party caucus room.

I sorted out my mistake with George's office, but he did have to share.

❖

I lost a second friend to breast cancer when Beth Gleeson died. My best friend, Maxene Hewitt, had died from the same horror in 1983. Beth's illness was diagnosed in 1988, not long before the election. She was the second of the eight women in the lower house of the Labor Caucus to develop this insidious disease. Pauline Toner was diagnosed with breast cancer not long before Beth was. I am convinced that the illness was triggered in both women by extreme stress. For Pauline, her failure to gain a Cabinet position after the 1985 election, due to factional machinations, was extremely stressful. She told me once that losing her Cabinet position was the worst thing that had ever happened to her. Beth's stress was the continual battle to hold her seat against opponents from within the Labor Party. Thomastown was like a ripe cherry waiting to be plucked by anyone who could reach it.

Pauline Toner died in March 1989, and Beth Gleeson died in December 1989. The loss of two of the eight Labor women in the Legislative Assembly in the 51st Parliament was a high price to pay for women's participation in politics.

Peter Bachelor was elected to Thomastown at the by-election following Beth's death, and took his seat at the autumn sitting of Parliament in 1990. He paid tribute to Beth in his inaugural speech, and I reproduce some of it here to honour the role Beth played as one of the pioneer women in the Victorian Parliament.

'Beth Gleeson recognised the needs of the outer suburban fringe, the needs of the suburbs and the needs of the families that live in them. She worked hard for the physical infrastructure, community amenities and human services so vital to the Thomastown electorate. I pay my personal tribute

*to Beth Gleeson and join with all members of Parliament,
as we did on 6 March, in expressing my deep sympathy to
Beth's family, her husband Mike, and daughters, Megan and
Lisa.'*

❖

I had less time available for committee work in my second term,
because of the job of Whip, and because my electorate work
seemed to be expanding exponentially. I felt like the guardian of
the people and services in my electorate, and behaved parochially
towards it. Someone called me the 'matriarch of Wantirna'. I
enjoyed the label.

I served on the Council of the Outer Eastern College of
TAFE — now part of Swinburne University. I demonstrated the
need for university facilities as well as TAFE in the Outer East,
and was a member of the first Board of Swinburne University,
with a campus under construction in Lilydale, now closed by
the Victorian Liberal-National Party Government.

I lobbied for a tram extension along Burwood Highway to
Knox. It finally arrived at Vermont during my third term in
Parliament. Expansion of bus routes, railway station improvement,
and road duplication were important issues to my constituents,
as Wantirna's population, in a developing outer urban region,
swelled — fast.

I retained my passion for housing policy, and chaired the
Ministerial Advisory Committee on Women and Housing.
We produced an important report, *Speaking of Housing*,
which presented the views of women all over Victoria on what
housing meant to them. Planning was underway for some of

the recommendations to be implemented, but was abandoned when the Kennett Liberal government won the next election in 1992.

❖

On January 25 1989, a few months after the election in which Labor scraped home with a three seat majority in the Legislative Assembly, Victoria was still in holiday mode. The Australian open tennis championship was being played in the new tennis centre that Premier John Cain had fostered. Pat Cash and Stefan Edberg played in the 16th round.

The Labor government was not travelling well. Deregulation of the Australian financial system had given free rein to a bunch of 'corporate cowboys' who borrowed from willing lenders to irresponsible excess. Australia was moving towards a recession, the one 'we had to have' according to Federal treasurer Paul Keating. A series of financial spot fires broke out in Victoria, starting with a 'scandal' about management of the Victorian Economic Development Corporation, (VEDC), in Deputy Premier Robert Fordham's Department. Companies financed with venture capital by the VEDC had lost $2 million. Given that the purpose of the VEDC was to provide venture capital for companies to establish themselves, $2 million does not seem a great deal. However, the government was unable to control the politics of the issue, despite Robert Fordham resigning on 31 January 1989.

The next financial disaster, the collapse of the Pyramid building society in Geelong should not have been a problem for government but a few months prior to the collapse, Attorney

General Andrew McCutcheon and Treasurer Rob Jolly had issued a press release supporting Pyramid and encouraging investors. The Farrow Group, directors of Pyramid, had pulled the wool over their eyes as well as fleecing the public.

The unsustainable debt position of merchant bank Tricontinental Corporation Ltd, the commercial arm of the Government-owned State Bank of Victoria, (SBV), became public early in 1990. The collapse of Tricontinental, with losses more than 3.5 times greater than the value of SBV's capital, causing the SBV to lose around $3 billion, brought about the collapse of the State Bank. This led to the resignation of Treasurer Rob Jolly on April 2, 1990. I remember Rob Jolly's distress after his resignation. Politics takes no account of feelings as it rolls savagely over its participants. On the same day Evan Walker, Government leader in the Legislative Council also selflessly resigned, to free up Cabinet positions, with the hope that a free Cabinet spot would stop the bickering that was taking place.

The government seemed to freeze after this. Because Cabinet decision-making was consensual rather than by majority vote, it was easy for Cabinet members seeking change in the leadership to prevent decision making by refusing to agree to anything.

John Cain resigned on 10 August 1990, his leadership untenable. As John walked from the Caucus room following his speech, the personal pain and the ruthlessness of politics hit me again. Following two days of bitter number crunching between Steve Crabb and Joan Kirner, the Caucus elected Joan as leader and hence Premier. I wondered whether things would have ended differently for the Government that started out with such ideals had Steve Crabb won that vote.

The SBV was sold to the Commonwealth Bank in August

1990, following the resignation of John Cain and the election of Joan Kirner as Premier.

❖

I had to find some humour as the crisis unfolded. I engaged in some banter with an Age columnist, about women and tools. On 12 September 1989 I wrote in response to an article denigrating shifting spanners. He followed with this article, which lightened my mood for a time.

> *Oops! We seem to have got on the wrong side of Carolyn Hirsh with our story last week taking the Michael out of a TV advertisement that portrays an 'A grade mechanic' performing heart surgery on a car while using shifting spanner. Why, we wondered, is this dill not using the proper tools of his trade? What is wrong with the ring spanner? An open- ended spanner? A ratchet socket drive?*

> *Down on us like a ton of environmentally sound adobe came the MLA for Wantirna. "I must take issue with your disparaging remarks about shifters and their uses," thundered Mrs Hirsh.*

> *"As a woman headed household for some 16 years, a shifter has been the mainstay of my toolbox. In fact, along with a hammer, a saw, a shovel, a couple of screwdrivers and a pair of tweezers, it has totally comprised my toolbox … shifters are absolutely indispensable for home maintenance because of their versatility."*

"I did make some concessions to expanding my 'kit' when I built the back fence. On that occasion I added soap (to lubricate the nails) and a crowbar (to dig the post holes) … I must admit that since one of my daughters moved out of home, taking the hammer with her, I have been reduced to using a meat tenderiser to bang in nails. However, since my daughters tend to come and go a bit, I expect that the hammer will turn up again.

"To suggest that shifting spanners are a tool of the incompetent is to malign the many competent and efficient home maintenance experts in our community. Let's hear it for the shifter (and for that matter, for the pliers)."

Indeed ma'am this cowardly column will quickly agree. The last place we want to find ourselves is before the bar of the house … and you standing before us with the shifter in your hand.

❖

On 13 August 1991 the late Brian Mier, Minister for Consumer Affairs and Aboriginal Affairs, resigned from Cabinet. Brian was a member of the Left so his resignation created a vacancy for a candidate from the Left. I tried to step into the vacancy — I had developed confidence in my ability to do the job, and saw the promotion as a logical step in my career. However, numbers rule in politics, and I was not successful. Tony Sheehan entered Cabinet, and in early 1992 replaced Tom Roper as Treasurer.

As well as upheaval in parliament, the Victorian Electoral

Commission undertook a redistribution of Legislative Assembly seats. I squeezed through the crowd in the library to see the maps of the new boundaries the day they came out and discovered that the Northern, labor-voting, half of my electorate of Wantirna, and the Southern half of the Ringwood electorate, which had been abolished, were combined to create a new seat of Bayswater. The eastern, labor-voting section of Wantirna had been moved into Knox electorate. Wantirna had moved south to become predominately a Liberal voting area. *Ah, Bayswater will do me,* was my immediate reaction. However, that didn't eventuate. Kay Setches, who was the Member for Ringwood, and a Minister by this time, won preselection for Bayswater, while I settled on my own electorate of Wantirna.

In August 1992 Steve Crabb announced that he would not contest his seat of Knox, which he had held for the Labor Party since 1976, so I decided to seek preselection for that electorate. While Wantirna seemed unwinnable, Knox had a five percent margin. *Perhaps I could win it.*

'Don't do it.' Steve Crabb advised me. 'Stay and contest Wantirna.'

Of course, he had seen Labor Party polling which showed that even Knox was as likely to fall to the Liberal Party as Wantirna was.

I took no notice of him, and Knox fell with a 10 percent swing to the Liberal Party

All the other Outer East Members lost their seats too, in a landslide to the Liberal-National Party. *That's it. It's over. I'm a failure. I've lost the job I loved.* These thoughts mixed with my tears as I sat on the edge of my bed at midnight on election night.

CHAPTER 10

THE SURPRISE ELECTION

I was wrong of course. I shouldn't have tried to predict the future. Ten years after a devastating election loss I found myself back in the Victorian Parliament in a new era. My earlier rejection was simply politics, even though it had felt personal. Politics doesn't discriminate between who it chews up and who it boosts onto a pedestal. Election wins and losses usually have little to do with the candidate and are mainly brought about by the status of their party in the electorate at the time.

The Labor Party hosted an exuberant barbecue the day after the 2002 election, my political rebirth — rife with hugs, handshakes, kisses and backslapping. I joined in. I recall the event, but with no feeling this time.

The few weeks after the election were a rush and a blur. I must have behaved normally. I arrived in the Community Services Department staffroom at the Chisholm Institute of TAFE as usual on the Monday after the election.

'Congratulations,' my colleagues were excited.

'Now you'll be able to do something about the conditions we work under.'

'We'll start lobbying you for more funding.'

'We'll miss you though.'

I'd gone to Chisholm to resign from my job — teaching social policy, counselling and community development subjects to Diploma students. The resignation had to take place before the official declaration of the election result. I packed up my desk, this time without a sense of failure.

❖

I made the first speech of my new life at the declaration of the poll — where the returning officer for the electorate officially announces the winner of the election. As I thanked the electoral office staff and Labor Party members, I noticed the previous Member, whom I'd defeated. She showed courage in turning up; she appeared close to tears — I knew how she felt. I had lost more elections than I'd won.

Declaration of the poll for Silvan Province 2002

There was an induction day in Parliament House for new Members a short time after the election. My young colleagues were wide eyed. Parliamentary staff organised our changeover from private citizen to public representative with a one day in-service — unheard of after my earlier elections. Someone gave me the anachronistic gold pass for Silvan Province that provided free train travel for Members. Introduced before cars and planes were the norm, it disappeared in 2006. In a nod to today's travel mode, Members were provided with a car by the Parliament — we'd used our own cars in the 1980s.

'Stand in front of the screen please.'

I joined the queue for photographs, printed onto sheets so staff could identify Members by name, and due to heightened security, copied onto swipe passes for identification and to enable access to Parliament House. When I was first elected in 1985, Members and staff were issued with keys, which could easily be copied. There was an 'urban myth' suggesting that half of Melbourne's population had keys to Parliament House, and that strange people roamed the bluestone corridors late at night.

One of the greatest changes I noticed in the ten years since I'd been a Member before was the intensified security arrangements. It was post 'nine-eleven', and security personnel carried guns this time. Visitors had to pass through scanners — no more wandering in through the front door.

'Who are you employing as your electorate officer?' Don asked me. Donald Barker had been my campaign director for the two Federal elections I'd contested — and lost — in 1996 and 1998. Upper house State Members were only allocated one staff member, to manage the office in the electorate. There was no staff allowance for backbench Members in their Parliament House offices.

'Do you want the job?' I asked Don, with some trepidation. I couldn't imagine Don managing the diverse role of an electorate officer.

'No, but Helen would like a change from her job.' I knew Helen was an extremely successful office administrator, so snapped her up.

Helen demonstrated her efficiency as we moved into the electorate office in Ringwood, and she exhibited unwavering loyalty over the next four years as I destroyed what I had.

Upper house Members of Parliament don't usually become heavily involved with constituents' problems, considered the job of lower house representatives. However, the Silvan Province office location halfway between Eastland shopping centre and the Ringwood bus and railway station encouraged passers-by with predicaments of all sorts to come in for help.

'Could you tell me where the vacuum cleaner shop is please?'

'Those TV towers must not go ahead.'

'I have nowhere to sleep tonight.'

'Do you have bus timetables?'

'Could I have a glass of water please?'

'I need a hip replacement and have to wait a year. Can you help?'

Another reason for the profusion of contacts with the office was my ongoing involvement with housing issues. Because of the perennial shortage of affordable housing, people came from both within and outside the electorate, hoping I could find them somewhere to live. Sometimes I could; most of the time I couldn't. Many problems that confronted us weren't to do with the State Government, and sometimes they could be resolved with a cup of tea and a listening ear.

I remember Arthur,* a sad man in his late forties, with a slight intellectual disability, who'd lived with his parents all his life. His father had died a few years before.

'My mum has died and my brother is selling the house. I don't know what to do.'

He was engulfed in grief, and devastated. He took to coming into the office every couple of days. I think he saw us, two older women, as surrogate mothers.

'You need to be a social worker as well as an office manager in this job,' Helen said.

I eventually found him a unit in a local seniors' public housing complex. He loved it, and the other residents loved him. He would fix and carry things for them, and became part of their extended families.

❖

My first caucus (Parliamentary Labor Party) meeting proved an agreeable surprise. I pushed open the narrow double doors and walked into the familiar caucus room, Room K, amidst a crowd of young spirited new and experienced Parliamentary Labor Party Members. I looked around. The two floor-length sash windows were still there, framed with drapes and leading onto little stone balconies. If a couple of Members wanted a private discussion, they would slide a window up and step outside. A morning shaft of sunlight from one window, like a spotlight, briefly illuminated a river of floating dust motes. The other window looked out on the garden and the grass tennis court. Australian landscape paintings, on loan from the National

---

* Not his real name

gallery still adorned the walls. 'Giant Gums' by Edward Cairns Officer drew me in among the trees as it shone with Australian light. The incongruous phone booth was gone from the corner of the room. There was no longer a need for it, since everyone had mobile phones — to be turned off during caucus meetings. Rob Hulls, a modern day Tom Roper or Steve Crabb, told us a warning story about a noisy phone that had been tossed into a jug of water.

The rows of chairs were the same, and I drifted to my familiar spot from ten years before. It was as if no time had elapsed, except for the people. Some I knew; others were unfamiliar. Some would have been still at school during my last stint, younger than my children were. Then I spotted George Seitz, close to my age, sitting in the same spot as ten years before, clinging to his seat like a limpet, as permanent as the bluestone walls.

The Premier and deputy leader took their places at the heavy polished table in front of the rows of Labor Members of Parliament. I felt as if I was in a time warp. So familiar, but last time I was there, Steve Bracks had been making his first two attempts to enter the Victorian Parliament and John Cain was Premier.

We new Members were welcomed with warm applause by those who'd been elected to the first Bracks government formed in 1999. I compared this caucus meeting with my first one in 1985. This one was like sitting in a field of flowers, rather than the rock-filled quarry of the earlier experience.

I was sworn in as a member of the Legislative Council on 25 February 2003, and found myself ensconced on a red velvet seat in that illustrious chamber, a bastion of male landowners since 1851. I looked around the chamber, considered architecturally to be one of the top six parliamentary chambers in the world. The same size as the Legislative Assembly, the Council chamber looks smaller because of the temple-like appearance created by rows of Roman Corinthian columns along each side of the room. The President's chair is surrounded by an elaborate canopy of scallop shells, laurel leaves and symbols of the British royal coat of arms. There is a story that the first woman elected to represent the Labor Party in the Legislative Council presented a Christmas felicitation speech — a poem she'd written herself — while sitting on top of the President's canopy. The red velvet upholstery — rather faded by my time — serves to heighten the royal connection. Lashings of gold leaf from Victorian gold rush days add richness to the decoration. One of my late night fantasies was that I would scrape it off and distribute it to homeless people. Rows of plaster molds of winged babies, not cherubs, but a secular version called *putti*, decorate the walls, while above them, bare breasted molded women represent the virtues of Victorian England. I suggested that at night the babies might fly up and suckle at the breasts of the women. Only some people laughed.

My seat in the Legislative Council 2003

❖

I was well regarded in this 'new generation' Labor Party caucus, considered an elder statesman, whose opinions were valued. Local lower house members would call into my office, next to the Legislative Council chamber, with its view of a brick wall covered with drainpipes.

'Carolyn, would you look over this speech please?'

'Whatever is the grievance debate?'

'Come and have a coffee.'

I was proud to be appointed by the Parliament to the Drugs and Crime Prevention joint Parliamentary Committee, and to be elected its Chair.

I began my second 'inaugural speech' with:

> '...As I was saying before I was so rudely interrupted some 10 years ago...'

I enjoyed preparing and presenting this speech — a unique opportunity to roam over a broad range of issues, and to acknowledge significant people in the Labor Party and my life

> ...I find [the Upper House] very different from my previous experience in what I could colloquially term 'the people's house' – the Legislative Assembly – in the 50th and 51st parliaments between 1985 and 1992. This is most illustrious, with its cherubs, velvet and gold. It is a very beautiful place...
>
> ...Neither my father, Peter Murphy, nor my mother, Dorothy, could...vote for representatives in this chamber

when I was a child. That is…extraordinary—that the privilege and limits to democracy… have continued for so long.

…I am one of the Murphys of Piangil – and I am very proud to be one of the Murphys of Piangil and to be in this place. My great-grandfather Michael Murphy came to Australia from Mallow in County Cork in 1840. He was from a landless, poor, Irish family.

And my great-grandmother Catherine Toland arrived on one of the so-called orphan ships, the Lady Kennaway, on 13 December 1848. She was with other young Irish women from the workhouses, and when they arrived here, they were called barefoot trollops and were treated extremely poorly by the society of the day. So you cannot see those people being part of this, then undemocratic, chamber…

…I want to finish by…talking about constitutional reform. I am looking forward to being a part of this chamber during this historical period of final democratisation, when this chamber will finally remove the last of the privileges that prevent proper representation – that is, every member will need to face the people at every election, as is proper in a democratic society…

❖

The next eighteen months were loaded with work — dealing with constituents in the electorate, attending functions with my Legislative Assembly colleagues, preparing and participating in Parliamentary debates, and working on the Drugs and Crime Prevention Committee with Sandy Cook, and Pete Johnston, the Executive Officer and Legal Research Officer. I loved working with these talented staff, and found the Committee the most satisfying part of my job.

We completed an enquiry into Amphetamine and 'Party Drug' Use in Victoria, incomplete from the previous Parliament. It was an interesting reference. I knew little about so-called 'party drugs' and less about the use of amphetamines as a drug of choice by drug users instead of heroin. The committee framed the recommendations around supply reduction measures, demand reduction measures and harm reduction measures, matching the platform of the National Drug Strategy. The committee made 89 recommendations in the broad areas of law enforcement and supply control; education and training; harm minimisation and harm reduction; partnerships and networking; the role of the media; policy, treatment and service delivery; specific groups; rural and regional issues; ongoing research; and funding. It was a comprehensive report, which I hope still informs policy development in Australia and overseas almost a decade later.

An early experience of the difference between the Cain government of the 1980s and the Bracks government of the 21st century occurred when I attempted to organise a press conference to launch my committee's report into *Amphetamine and 'Party Drug' Use in Victoria*. It had always been task of a particular committee to organise a press conference shortly after its report was tabled in Parliament. When I started this process I was confronted by a 'whirling dervish' of Sharon McCrohan, then Government media office chief, who told me, in no uncertain terms that the Government, not Parliamentary Committees, organised press conferences.

Eventually we reached a compromise. I recall sitting at a computer in the government media office writing a press release, while a couple of media advisers watched over my shoulders and edited my work as I went. I was astonished, but this incident exemplified the control that the Bracks government exerted over the Parliamentary Labor Party. No wonder caucus meetings were so friendly — they were more like social occasions. There were few disagreements in caucus. Compliant caucus committees had already approved policies and bills by the time they came to caucus.

With Gough Whitlam at a Labor Party Function 2003

❖

I attended Labor Party functions as often as I could during the first year-and-a-half of this surprise term. I was, and still am, grateful for the privilege of serving in the Victorian Parliament, which would not have happened without the endorsement of the Labor Party.

However, as well as the locked door behind which I'd shoved the horror of Vicki's death, along with concomitant emotions, values and judgment, physical health problems interfered with my new job as a Member of Parliament. A few months after my daughter's suicide, pain began stalking me. I was bringing up my granddaughter, Jessica, who had lost her mother, as I had lost my daughter. I had moved from Boronia to Glen Iris shortly before Vicki's death to be close to Jessica's parents and her school, which meant though, I lost easy access to my family and network of friends in the Outer East. Jessica had just completed year ten when I was elected, and I somehow managed to continue to cook meals, and drive Jessica to and from part-time jobs, sporting and social events most of the time.

I knew about pain. After all, I'd given birth to three children and lived a busy life for over 65 years. I had a theory about it. My theory didn't help the pain, but the operations did.

CHAPTER 11
LIFT WHEN I SAY

This physical pain was more insidious than any I'd experienced, but its nature was familiar. I'd lie awake at night trying to find a comfortable position as my hip bones grated together. My mind would drift to the back pain I'd experienced some time after my husband, Peter's sudden death 30 years before — pain that felt the same — that left me wrestling for a spot in bed that would allow me to sleep. It hadn't been caused by stress, but by creating a garden from the clay-covered building site around the new house I'd moved into in 1973 three weeks after his death.

❖

'Lift when I say. One, two, three, heft.'

It was a strain but I managed my end of the railway sleeper,

Stephen, the other. We placed it on top of the stack of three. I'd bought forty red gum sleepers, discarded by the railways, to build a retaining wall. Stephen, a friend I taught with at school, was helping.

It was a year or two after my children and I had moved into our new home, which was supposed to be our dream home. Peter and I had planned it with pleasure over the previous few years, but it had not turned out that way. I was managing the task of building a garden bit by bit, on my own. After all, I was young and fit, only thirty-six, and I had been off cigarettes for almost a year. I built a fence without help, digging postholes with a crowbar and a mattock. It was still standing twenty years later when I moved away.

I started on the retaining wall — managed to heft a few sleepers into place, but they were too heavy, and my back ached — hence Stephen's help for the weekend. We finished the wall, one and a half metres from a side fence, four sleepers high. Eventually the raised garden behind it became a feature, filled with every species of fern I could find.

However, the fence and the retaining wall had painful consequences. A fortnight after we completed the retaining wall, I arrived at school and reached into the boot to retrieve a box of books. Something in my back cracked and I could not straighten up. I had developed a ubiquitous *bad back*, and made my first and only workers' compensation claim. Although the injury manifested itself at work, I was sure that lifting the sleepers and building the fence had set it off. There was no argument with the workers' compensation people though, as bad backs were rife in those days when occupational health and safety laws were not even a twinkle in the legislators' eyes.

I went to every back expert I could find and followed

up different theories of treatment. I eventually cured it by swimming — gradually increasing my first panting two laps with rests along the way, to forty laps a day, most mornings for years. Finally, bored with looking at the bottom of the pool — black lines, the odd band-aid — I took up aqua-aerobics, which I found much more fun.

Regular cycling became part of my exercise repertoire in the early 1980s. It was over 20 years since I'd been on a bicycle, nine months pregnant, riding to the shops to buy our Friday night treat of fish and chips and apple cider. Vicki had been born two days later, and the bicycle rusted in the shed.

The most exciting ride I participated in after I started cycling again was a sixteen-day trip from the Blue Mountains to Melbourne with Bicycle Victoria. The organisation provided support, and the thousand participants camped each night on a football oval somewhere. I can still conjure up yellow days on narrow country roads, sun, breeze wafting on my face, paddocks of grass hay ready for harvest, and silence except for the swish of tyres on tarmac.

❖

My exercise regime fell into disarray as Vicki's mental illness grew progressively worse, and I took on the care of my granddaughter, Jessica, for ongoing periods. I gave up my psychology practice, because my own emotional troubles were overwhelming me. I probably needed to swap places with my clients. I took a final decision about my private practice when I converted my office into a bedroom for Jessica. I kept up teaching at Chisholm TAFE though — I needed the income, and the work was easier.

I put on some weight, and my back extracted its next payment for the railway sleepers and the fence all those years before. My feet developed permanent numbness. Three months after Vicki's death I developed severe pain in my left groin. Groin strain, I thought, like the footballers, but I was wrong. It was hip pain due to osteoarthritis, which stripped away the cartilage between the ball and socket of the hip joint. My health spiralled downwards. The more pain I was in, the less I exercised, and so on. I exacerbated the problem by putting on lots of weight — twenty kilos, which led to symptoms of type-two diabetes. I was sixty-three at the time of Vicki's death, an age when I should have been taking more care of my health, not less.

Arthritis is an autoimmune disease, and I believe it attacked me so suddenly because of my body's retention of the stress related hormone, cortisol, which interfered with my immune system. Humans are still biologically primitive beings. We produce cortisol when we experience the 'fight-flight response', for example when we are attacked by a sabre-toothed tiger, or nearly have a car smash. It enhances our bodily functions and responses. We often feel tired after experiencing a big fright, as the body's relaxation response is activated and washes the extra cortisol from our system. Prolonged stress without relaxation leads to ongoing release and retention of cortisol, which has been shown to cause a range of health problems. These can include impaired cognitive performance, blood sugar imbalances, lowered immunity and inflammatory responses in the body. I did nothing about the emotions I had crammed away, despite knowing this physiology, and I paid a physical price.

My right hip became so painful I had difficulty walking, and I had to stop taking anti-inflammatory tablets, as they were eating the lining of my stomach — ugh!

'Oh dear, bone on bone,' the orthopedic surgeon said as he looked at the x-rays.

I had been booked for a hip replacement a few months hence. When I won the election late in 2002, I brought the operation forward to January 2003, so I would not miss any of the first session of Parliament. As it was, I was still using a stick on 25 February 2003, the first day of the 55th Parliament.

The hip replacement was successful. I have experienced no more problems in my right hip, then or since, but the arthritis began to gnaw at the cartilage around my left hip. I had a second hip replacement two years later.

Almost the only joints not affected by arthritis at that stage were my knees, but I fixed that when I fell while chasing the cat down the steps trying to catch it to give it a tablet. I injured my left knee and it did not get better, possibly because, as with my mental health difficulties, I did not seek treatment. As soon as I fell, and my knee began to resemble a time-lapse film of a pumpkin growing, I did sit with it raised and iced. I was a few minutes into that, when my cousin, Joanne, rang from Gosford, on the New South Wales Central Coast.

'Aunty Nan is about to die, and I can't stand it anymore Caro. You have to come up.'

Our much-loved Aunty Nan, my mother's sister, had no children, so we cousins looked after her as she aged.

'I'll be there as soon as I can.' I could not refuse to go.

I caught a flight to Sydney, a train to Gosford and a taxi to the hospital. I arrived about midnight, my knee a lump of molten lava. I sent my exhausted cousin home and held Aunty Nan's hand until about 4 am, a time the nurse said many people close to death let go. But our darling aunt did not die that night.

Instead, she opened her eyes, still with their sapphire shine.

'Hello Caro,' she said. 'What are you doing here?'

She didn't die until a few days later. I was glad I was there.

But I had ignored my knee. I tried some treatment after I arrived back home, but it was not successful, so in July 2005 I underwent a left knee replacement.

The arthritis continued its insidious attack on my body, relishing the cartilage around the vertebrae in my lower back, weakened by the earlier injury. The numbness in my feet increased to a point where I found it difficult to balance, and took to a permanent walking stick. A referral to the 'best back man in Melbourne' led to a recommendation for more surgery. I did not have it. I decided not to replace any more of my human flesh with artificial parts, preferring numb feet to another operation.

Ongoing descriptions by old people about their operations and general health problems are generally unedifying. However, I include this chapter to demonstrate first, that a great deal of physical stress accompanied the untreated emotional and mental stress I was under during my third term in Parliament, and second, to set the scene for the hypothesis I have developed to explain, at least in part, an addiction to poker machines I developed.

❖

The agony I experienced in my hips and my left knee completely disappeared once an orthopedic surgeon had replaced them with artificial joints made of titanium, steel and porcelain. My mobility increased and I could hardly remember the level of pain I had suffered, so perhaps my subconscious mind picked up an idea that mechanically induced physical pain relief could translate into mechanically induced emotional pain relief.

Perhaps since substituting real pieces of me with mechanical bits had fixed my physical agony, I attempted to substitute the unresolved grief, guilt, and shame I had locked within me with a mechanical solution — the hypnotic mindlessness of poker machines — in the hope that I might remove that misery.

The addiction to alcohol that I also developed during this period added a chemical component of 'pain replacement', which replaced the anti-inflammatory medication I'd used to keep physical pain at bay. However, the facile explanation I invented to justify the dual addictions I developed fell apart when I realised that while I had consulted specialists about my physical ills, I did not do so about the emotional agony I carried. I regret that I didn't. I might have avoided the snowball of shame and humiliation that rolled over my family and me through the next few years.

I have labelled the addictions that attacked me 'illnesses'. While most theories suggest that they are, there are questions. Is addiction illness, bad habit, or weak willpower? I'm not sure — perhaps it is a combination of all three. However there is no doubt that addiction changes the chemistry of the brain, perhaps permanently. The suggestion that complete and permanent abstinence from any addictive behaviour is the only way to be sure of preventing a relapse, argues for the permanence of brain changes brought about by addiction.

While I underwent successful joint replacement for illness and injury, I accepted at last that I couldn't deal with mental health problems by 'brain replacement' with the mind-numbing mechanical and chemical solutions I attempted.

CHAPTER 12
CAUGHT AGAIN

Whatever happened to me? A Member of Parliament making the law and breaking it. I'd always thought myself a law-abiding citizen, and had tried to instill these values in my children. But when I locked my emotions away because I found them too awful to face, I locked my values and respect for the law away with them.

Later, when I unlocked the door, and began to draw out hidden horrors, some of the beliefs and values locked away with them trickled back into my consciousness. With them emerged one of my earliest memories that taught me my first understanding of right and wrong.

❖

I stand in my grandpa's bungalow at the end of a brick path in the back yard of our house in Thornbury. I feel a little shiver of excitement. I am breaking a rule. I have been told not to go into Grandpa's room unless he asks me, but the door is not shut properly and I have slipped through. I have been in here plenty of times before with Grandpa, when he reads me stories, but never on my own. It is quiet and no one knows I'm here. I grab at a river of dust dancing in the sunlight.

My mother is busy with my new little brother in the house, and quite distracted. He is my birthday present. I turned three the day he arrived. I am allowed to hold him when my mother says I can. He is so soft, with tiny hands that wrap themselves around my finger. He smells beautiful, except when he does a big stinky poo in his nappy. I don't. I do poo and wee in my pot. I look under Grandpa's bed. Yes, he has a pot too — a big one. We all have one under our beds, except my new baby.

There is a dark brown chest of drawers in front of me, much taller than I am. The drawers have wooden knobs. When I stand back near the door, on tiptoes, I can see something glinting on top of the chest. I want to have a proper look at what is on top. I think I know what it is. I can't quite see what's there, but I know there are lollies in a glass jar, because Grandpa gives me one when I visit him. They are different colours and lovely to suck, especially the red ones.

I climb up onto Grandpa's big bed, and can see the lolly jar. I can see my nursery rhyme book too, that Grandpa has been reading to me. It has a funny picture of Humpty Dumpty on the cover. I can't reach from the bed though, it's too far away.

I climb down from the bed and see the bottom drawer is a little bit open. I pull and it opens a bit further. I pull the next one open. I climb onto the bottom drawer, then reach up with one foot to the next drawer. Then I feel myself falling backwards as the huge chest of drawers tips over on top of me.

I scream and howl. I'm stuck under the giant cupboard. My mother rushes in, lifts the edge and I crawl out, still howling. My mother hugs me then smacks me.

I do not go into my grandpa's bungalow on my own again.

❖

After my first transgression of drink driving in June 2004, I became more depressed. My job as a Member of Parliament had been wonderful. I had been able to pretend, to some degree, that I was back in the 1980s. I had been able to block out the emotions that I was too afraid to feel, but the infringement and the punishment — the loss of my Committee — and the public shame forced me to face a degree of reality. Vicki was dead and I was rearing her daughter, Jessica. I was no longer the wise elder to whom new Members of Parliament came for advice. My Legislative Assembly friends, newly elected in marginal seats, avoided me. I still attended some functions, but fewer, partly because I felt too humiliated, partly so as not to embarrass other Members and Ministers by my presence.

I still kept my emotions locked in that dark place they'd been since Vicki's death in 2001. The task became more difficult though as shame and humiliation joined the grief and guilt I could not bear.

❖

I was managing public transport and taxis reasonably successfully, but, time permitting, I would spend an hour or so between trams in a poker machine venue nearby. They were everywhere and 'pokies' and a glass or two of wine became my friends.

It helps break up the journey and it makes me feel better. I told no one about this activity, which did make me feel better while I was in the thrall of the lights, colours and music. It helped me to lock out unwanted thoughts. This period was the start of the insidious relationship with poker machines and alcohol that took over my life.

Politics is a bit like the ocean. Endless waves wash up, obliterating evidence of earlier waves. The sand retains little of its shape before the last tide. My transgression faded from the minds of the media and my colleagues. As far as everyone believed, it was over. The next election was still two and a half years away, and the Premier had implied I could rejoin 'my' committee the following year. All I had to do was use public transport for six months. However, like the unpredictability of the ocean, no one knows what will happen next in politics. A wave rolled from a different direction and slammed into me.

There were two representatives in each Legislative Council Province at that time, elected at alternate elections. The other Silvan Province Member was a Liberal, Andrew Olexander. About a month after my drink-driving transgression, in July 2004, he crashed his Parliamentary car into three other cars early one morning in Port Melbourne, and caused about $100,000 damage. He recorded a blood alcohol level well over the legal limit of .05 BAC. The media loved it, and of course, as well as reporting his behaviour, all media outlets revisited and replayed my first transgression, linking it to my colleague. I had to live through another serve of shame and humiliation. For example, one media outlet said,

'The idiocy of drink-driving ought to be plainly obvious to

parliamentarians such as Ms Hirsh and Mr Olexander.'

The media enjoyed the irony of drink driving transgressions from both Members for Silvan Province; a wag suggested there might be something strange in the water of the Silvan Reservoir. Andrew Olexander's wrongdoing had been a lot more serious than mine had, but because the two were lumped together, they became equivalent. My emotional state reverted to that of the previous month, and again, I saw my transgression reflected in everyone's eyes.

I made up for being guilty of the lesser evil than my colleague in September, only two months later, when the police caught me driving unlicensed.

❖

My granddaughter Jessica was to turn eighteen on 5 October 2004. She had gained her learner's permit when she turned sixteen and her father taught her to drive. Her logbook had the necessary hours, and she was booked to sit her licence test the day after her birthday.

My daughter, Teresa, rang me.

'Mum, Geoff's bought a ute. You know his old car, the brown Hornet. He doesn't need it anymore. We thought Jessie could have it.'

The brown Hornet was a 1989 Ford Laser, a manual car, which had proved reliable. I was pleased for Jessica. She would have wheels, albeit slow ones, once she gained her licence. Teresa and Geoff brought the car down to Glen Iris in early September for us to look after for the few weeks until Jessica 'got her Ps'.

To stop the battery going flat I started it most days and drove it up and down the drive. This was not a good idea, as the action somehow blurred a line for me between driving and not driving.

On the morning of 17 September I had an appointment at the Diabetes Institute in Caulfield. It wasn't far 'as the crow flies', but the trip took nearly an hour by public transport. I was running late, called a taxi, waited, grew impatient. When it did not turn up, I grabbed the keys and climbed into the brown hornet. *Just this once.*

I arrived for the appointment on time, to be told that my sugar levels were too high and I was verging on full-blown diabetes.

'Oh well,' I said. 'It doesn't matter. I don't really care.'

Shoulder shrugging words. Why did I not care? Why did I feel nothing? Why did I not get psychological help then?

I chugged back towards home in the brown Hornet. I passed a police car. The officer had pulled someone over. I didn't worry. I was creeping along anonymously in a little old brown car. The police officer would not be interested in me.

I had turned a corner when red and blue lights appeared behind me, a siren blared. The officer clearly wanted me to pull over. *How does he know I am breaking the law?* My stomach churned, my heart pounded, and I began to tremble as I stopped the car. I could feel emotion after all.

The police officer walked up to my window. I sat still, externally calm, inside a morass of seething horror.

'Do you have a reason for driving an unregistered car, Ma'am?' he asked.

'It's registered,' I replied.

'That label is out of date. By a month.'

The car was registered. I knew it had been paid. I might even have paid it, but Teresa and Geoff had not replaced the old label. After all, the car was not needed for another few weeks.

'It's been paid. The label is on the table. I'll put it on as soon as I get home.'

'Could I see your licence please Ma'am?' the police officer asked.

In my old, non-criminal life, I would have quietly explained that I'd done a stupid thing, and thrown myself on his mercy, but no, I compounded my law-breaking behaviour, piling deceit on deceit.

'I haven't got it with me,' I said.

'What is your name and address please?'

By this stage, I was completely irrational with fear. *How had this happened? What will I do?* I knew the car was still registered in my daughter's name and address.

'My name is Teresa O'Neale*. I live at…' I had just given the police officer my daughter's name and address.

He went back to his car. I contemplated driving off, but retained enough sanity to sit still.

The police officer came back to my window.

'What is your date of birth please, Ms O'Neale?'

'The fourteenth of October, 1964.' That was easy. Of course I remembered the date — after all, she was my daughter. The police officer gave me a strange look.

'I look older than I am, I've had a hard life,' I said.

Had I not been in the middle of a massive nervous breakdown I would have laughed at that remark. Instead I sat, trembling. The police officer disappeared to his car, came back with a camera and snapped a flash shot of me.

---

* Not her real name

'Please put the new registration label on the car, and take your licence to the nearest police station within seven days,' he said. I still had time to confess, but didn't. He drove off, and after a while, I drove shakily home.

Why had I done it? Why had I driven the car? Why had I lied to the police officer? That day I threw integrity, values, maturity and my competent adult self out a window. I felt as I had most of the time between the ages of ten and fourteen years. With even a small amount of rational thought, I could have sorted out most of what I had done, but my rationality disappeared under the same great slab of despair that had flattened me in my early adolescence. I sat under the weight. *I'm a criminal.* A memory flashed into my head of lawbreaking behaviour that had brought me into contact with the police when I was ten years old.

❖

Our neighbour's eighteen-month-old child died. It was sudden. I knew this little girl, Pamela,⋆ and I used to visit and play with her. She was so pretty, with red curls and she would hug me. Only my cat, Sooty, had ever died. He slept in a grave in the back yard, and I had collected pretty stones and made a border around it. Sometimes I sprinkled flowers on it. Little Pamela's death was a lot sadder, and I couldn't do anything about it.

I used to play in the cemetery, a typical country town cemetery, which was at the end of a path around the bend of the river. Sometimes my brothers would come too. We went there sometime after Pamela's death and I saw her grave. It was

---

⋆ Not her real name

not like most of the other graves, which were beautiful. They had glass domes filled with white flowers, bedspreads of white pebbles, concrete borders with clever designs, and statues of Jesus. Her little grave was covered with loose clay, with a board stuck in it. I knew it was Pamela's grave because I could see her name printed on the board with black paint.

This isn't fair. I gathered bits of beautiful decorations from the other graves — only those with lots. I arranged them on her grave and covered the clay with white stones. When I'd finished, it looked beautiful, and I went home, pleased to have done something for her.

Within a week, the local policeman appeared in our shop. He didn't want to buy anything, but spoke to my mother.

'Carolyn has stolen property from a number of graves in the cemetery,' he said to her. 'It is quite serious.'

My mother was furious, and made me go the cemetery and put everything back. I couldn't remember the proper place for some things, but in the end Pamela's grave was as bare as before. I cried while I did it, because I didn't realise that what I had done was wrong. I thought that the other graves had so many beautiful things, so that the people wouldn't mind sharing.

❖

This time, I was fully aware of the law-breaking nature of my behavior. I sat for a time on the edge of my bed, under the slab of despair, then panicked and caught public transport to my office in Ringwood. When I look back, I realise that had I stayed home, told no one, and contacted the police officer who had pulled me over, I might have been able to face the consequences of my behaviour without publicity. I may have been able to serve whatever penalty I received under the media's radar.

As soon as I arrived at my office, I told Helen, then rang the Caucus liaison officer, as I had three months earlier when I had blown .07. Why did I do that? Why didn't I ring a solicitor? The first time the media had been aware of my wrongdoing because journalists have police scanners that alert them to matters of interest. However, this misdemeanour would not have triggered the interest of the media, since neither my name nor my car had been involved. *I just need make sure the Premier knows. In case the media find out and ambush him.*

'I need you to tell the Premier what's happened, just in case the media get onto it, so he won't be caught unawares,' I told Lisa McDonald.

It didn't occur to me that the Premier and his staff would throw me to the wolves, that the Government Media Unit would initiate a media attack on me by issuing a release detailing my lawbreaking behaviour, along with a response from the Premier. Their reasoning was that they needed to control the situation and minimise damage to the Premier and the Government. I understood the Premier had to be seen to be tough, and he was very angry. *I should have kept my mouth shut.*

The Caucus Liaison Officer arrived with Andrew Giles, Labor Party Official and solicitor. I had an urgent need to confess my crime, so I asked them to come with me to the Boronia Police Station, where I made an informal statement about the illegal behaviour I had engaged in that morning. *Why didn't I keep my mouth shut?*

I can recall a crowd of people in my office later in the day — probably only three or four, but it felt like a crowd. Someone handed me a letter.

'You have to sign this,' they said.

It was a letter from me to the Labor Party State Secretary resigning from the Labor Party.

'No,' I said, 'No, I won't resign from the Party.'

I refused to sign it for some time — the Labor Party was part of my identity.

The phone rang. Someone handed me the receiver.

'It's the Premier for you,' they said.

'You have to resign.' I think he was shouting. He was insistent.

In the end, I signed the letter.

CHAPTER 13
LOST LONG AGO

I sat at my desk in my black leather chair in my electorate office. The Premier had shouted at me and I had resigned from the Labor Party. I was 67 years old. At the same time I was 11 years old sitting at a chipped green desk with a lift-up lid at Cressy State School, weeping while Tom Ryan, the headmaster shouted at me. How had I gone back there?

❖

It was Tuesday 14 August 1945.

I was a third grade pupil at Macedon State School, a two-teacher school of about thirty-five children. We had arrived at school at the usual time, and waited outside for Mr Russell, our Headmaster, to ring the bell. I can remember being puzzled, because we waited for much longer than usual.

'It's way after bell time,' Bob, a sixth grade boy said.

'And he's not even here yet,' my friend, Pat, said.

A little while later, Mr Russell ran across the road from his house.

'The war is over, the war is over,' he shouted and waved his arms as he ran.

'There's no school today or tomorrow,' Mr Russell told us. 'The Government has given us two days holiday to celebrate the end of the war, so everyone can go home.'

Trevor, a big sixth grade boy, rushed to the bell and pulled the rope. The bell rang out.

'Yes, you can all ring it — let everyone know the war is finished,' Mr Russell pulled the rope, and we all had a turn. Ringing the school bell was fun, and it pealed through the town for a long time.

I had turned eight a fortnight before, and didn't fully understand what the excitement was about, although I entered into it with the other children. I had some understanding of the war, gleaned from my grandmother.

❖

A few years earlier grandma had taken me into town where we had watched rows and rows of soldiers marching, with bands playing to keep them in time. I waved an Australian flag, and we all cheered. My grandmother spotted all her sons in the march. I couldn't understand why she cried.

Later, there was a celebration at Grandma's house, as all four uncles had leave before they went away again. My aunt Mary played the piano and my uncle Billy played a brass instrument

— it may have been a tuba. I sat under the dining room table and an uncle gave me an egg-cup full of beer.

The only other knowledge of the war I can recall is the image of the lawns around the Shrine of Remembrance dug up and formed into rows of trenches and heaps of clay.

'They're air raid shelters for us to hide in if the Japanese attack,' my grandmother had said.

Our family was lucky in this war. My father did not go, and my four uncles arrived home safely, whereas in the First World War one of my grandmother's brothers was killed during the battle of the Somme in France.

❖

After the bell ringing, we wandered home from school. Later in the day, townsfolk herded all of us children, even the little ones, to an open grassy area near the town, where a giant bonfire had been built. An effigy of Hitler sat on top, with a cornflakes packet for a head. We had cordial and biscuits while we watched the bonfire — it was a wonderful blaze. After it died down, we were allowed to shove potatoes, strung onto pieces of wire, into the hot coals around the edges of the bonfire. I can still taste the fluffy, white potato I found when I broke open the crust of charred skin.

The next day there was a procession along the main street. I wore a nurse's uniform my mother had made for my birthday, and stood, with other dressed-up children, on the back of a truck decorated with wattle. I felt very proud, as adults lining the street clapped while we passed. The parade was followed in the evening by a dance at the local hall, which the whole town attended. We children slid around the floor between dances.

❖

The celebration of the end of World War II epitomised my time at Macedon. I recall the three years we lived there as full of adventure and excitement. I played among gums and wattles on a bush block behind our house. A family of fairies lived under mushrooms and danced on the moss that carpeted the creek bank, and tadpoles in the creek hatched into green frogs. My friends and I pulled lumps of toffee-textured sap from wattle trees and chewed them. We filled our schoolbags with blackberries from the old quarry — my mother made them into jars of blackberry jam. We picked armfuls of yellow broome from bushes at the side of the road, to decorate cubby houses we built in the cyprus hedge along one side of our back yard. Our border-collie dog, Tippy, always accompanied my brothers and me on our adventures. I went to Sunday school each week, and of course attended school, which I loved.

I had skipped grade 2 when we moved from Melbourne to Macedon.

'Carolyn is well ahead of the other children, and she should go straight into grade 3,' Mr Russell, the headmaster, told my mother.

My parents had bought the general store at Macedon, and we lived in the attached two-roomed house behind the shop. My father converted a back veranda into a bedroom each for my brother and myself, lined with boards from fruit boxes. My younger brother slept in a cot in my parents' room. There was no bathroom; a bath sat on the cement-floored washhouse. It had no taps, so water was heated in the wood-fired copper and bucketed into the tub for the weekly bath. None of this mattered to me, but my mother was unhappy about the shack we lived in.

With my brothers, Alan and Kevin, Macedon 1946: Studio Portrait

My father bought a horse and cart to deliver groceries and stock feed to farms around the town. The horse was big and white, with hairy feet. His name was Bluey. Sometimes my father would let us ride on the cart while he did the deliveries. Later, when we 'came up in the world', he swapped the horse and cart for a T-model Ford utility.

'Come on Carolyn,' he would say during school holidays. 'You can help me deliver the groceries up the Mount.'

My father would stand, feet astride on the cart, shaking the reins and clucking 'horse language' at Bluey to encourage him up the steadily rising road. I would sit at the back, legs dangling.

'Up the Mount' was a euphemism for the weekly delivery of a cartload of goods to Yooralla. I loved going with him on this trip, but found it confronting. Yooralla was then a hospital school for children with physical disabilities, mainly children who had suffered polio during one of the epidemics. It was evacuated from Melbourne in 1942 for the duration of the war, to the Golf House, a magnificent old guesthouse at Mt Macedon. The Golf House was demolished in 1976.

The Golf House Mt. Macedon (Courtesy Wikimedia Commons)

The children there had irons on their legs, or lay in bath chairs. I would say hello to them, but I'd cry on the way home, because they were the same age as me. I wondered later whether these trips influenced my later decision to become a Special Education teacher, working with children with disabilities.

❖

On my 10th birthday, my mother my brothers and I left Macedon, and went to Grandmother's house at Windsor, in

Melbourne. We'd left our shop the previous day, and stayed overnight at a boarding house across the road. I had a room on my own on the first floor — we had to climb a flight of wooden stairs to a long verandah, from which the row of rooms opened. I found this very exciting, and even more so when I woke up on my birthday and looked out the door onto the verandah, at a magnificent sunrise. I believed God had sent the rainbow colours to me as a birthday present.

My mother, brothers and I stayed at my grandmother's for five months, and I do not recall that we saw our father during this time. I have never found out where he was. I did not attend school, and my brothers and I enjoyed the extended holiday. Tippy, our dog, stayed with us, and we taught him to walk in suburban streets while we held a rope tied to his collar. My grandmother would take us walking with Tippy to St Kilda beach. He had never seen waves before and he leaped through them, barking excitedly. These months at my grandmother's were familiar and pleasant — we had spent time there all our lives. Things weren't right though. My mother seemed to cry a lot, and she didn't seem to want me around her. I wondered what I had done wrong.

'Off you go Caro, out to play.'

'Shoo, we've grown-up things to talk about. Go and play with your brothers.'

'Go and finish reading that book I bought you Caro. Mum and I are talking.'

My aunts or my grandmother would close the door between my weeping mother and me.

My parents got back together with the purchase of a run-down general store at Cressy, in the Western district of Victoria, about two hours from Melbourne. We caught the train there, with Tippy in a box in the guard's van. My father was at the station to meet us when we arrived.

❖

Cressy was another world and another life. The house behind the shop was better in some respects than the one at Macedon, but much worse in other respects. As the only girl, I had a bedroom to myself. My brothers shared a sleep-out walled in on the back veranda. There was no washhouse, except on Mondays, when my mother lifted the lino-covered benches in the kitchen to expose cement troughs and another wood-fired copper. But there was a bathroom with a tap and a chip bath heater. We had come up in the world. We did not have mains water at Cressy. We relied on tanks on a tank-stand in the backyard, and water conservation became a permanent feature of our lives.

The first horrors we faced in the house at Cressy were fleas. They were in plague proportions throughout the house and the yard. If we stood still for more than 30 seconds, fleas would crawl up our legs. We found out that the previous owners had kept greyhounds, which spent their lives shedding fleas indoors and out. I don't know how my mother dealt with the fleas, but throughout our time at Cressy I would often find a flea or two in my bed. There were flea-ridden, rickety sheds at the back of the yard, unused I think. My father did not plant anything as he had at Macedon — the backyard grew brown grass.

There was no cyprus hedge for building cubbies. The shrubbery comprised prickly, unfriendly boxthorn bushes. There were no wattles, and the patch of grey gum trees across the road from our shop had no magic, only a humiliating track worn by my father as he walked to the hotel and back every day.

I have few memories of my mother during the early years at Cressy, except of her being cross with one or all of us. She never discussed it with me, but I found out in the end that my father had had an affair in Macedon, which devastated her. Nevertheless, she chose to do her duty. She moved to Cressy with my father, and took over running the shop when he had to get a job to make ends meet.

My father hid whatever shame, guilt or anger he may have felt by becoming an alcoholic.

He was secretary of the Cressy Football Club, and one night at a Saturday dance, when I was about sixteen, one of the club members came from the supper room behind the stage and told me my father had collapsed — I was so ashamed I ran home, climbed in my bedroom window and hid in the wardrobe. Kevin, the younger of my two brothers, eleven or twelve years old, helped my staggering, incoherent father through the hall in front of everyone, poured him into his ute, and drove him home.

❖

I went into grade six at Cressy State School. It was a two-room school like Macedon, but there were no more similarities. The headmaster, Tom Ryan, was a sadistic bully and I was frightened of him.

'What's seven sixes? Carolyn Murphy?' he would ask.

'Forty two plus eighty seven. Quickly, what's the answer? Carolyn Murphy?'

When I did not, or could not answer, he would dig the

knuckles of his second finger hard into my ribs, which hurt, and I would burst into tears.

'You are a retard, Carolyn Murphy,' he would say.

The more Mr Ryan bullied me, the more I cried.

There were two 'gangs' at Cressy State School and I was in neither. One gang ate their lunch in the shelter shed, the other on seats beside the basketball court. I ate my lunch sitting in the fork of tree branches across the schoolyard.

I was due to start at Colac High School the following year, with a ride back and forth each day between Cressy and Colac on the school bus. Mr Ryan spoke to my mother.

'Your daughter is retarded,' he said. 'She should stay at State School until she turns fourteen, then get a job in the box factory in Colac until she finds a husband.'

Luckily, my mother was wise enough to ignore Mr Ryan's advice, and enrolled me in form one (year seven) at Colac High School for the next year.

❖

I can still feel the shadow of fear that overwhelmed me the first morning at high school. New students had to sit a test. The teacher told us to bring a pencil in to the room. I didn't have one, so I sneaked away, hid behind some lockers and cried.

'Whatever is wrong?' A teacher found me some time later.

'I haven't got a pencil.'

The teacher took me into the room, and handed me a pencil and the test, although the time was almost up. Its purpose was to grade the form one students according to their scores. The children with the highest scores went into 1A, the next group into 1B, and the leftovers into 1C to undertake a modified curriculum suited to their poor test results. I was placed in 1C where it was expected that we would leave school when we turned fourteen and work in the box factory or its equivalent.

The 'A' stream undertook a 'professional' curriculum, comprising French, maths, English and English literature, history, geography and science. I am not sure what we did in 1C, but my teachers realised I had been wrongly placed and put me into 2A the next year. I made my first friend since we'd left Macedon, Jeannie Buckingham, who was new to the school in form two. My confidence improved somewhat, although I would still hide in the middle of a bush during sport time.

I have some pleasant memories: a maypole with plaited streamers for a May Day celebration; and physical education with Miss Duff for girls only. We undertook a series of exercises, and afterwards Miss Duff would instruct us to stand in a line facing a brick wall. She would explain the principles of good posture to us, and walk along the row patting our bottoms saying, 'Soft as butter, soft as butter, pull your bottom tight.' I can remember clenching my cheeks as tightly as I could, but she would still pat and make the same comment. Things were different then.

When I was fourteen and started form four, (year 10), I experienced a miracle. It equalled the fairies on the moss at Macedon, but it was real. A new teacher came to the school as Deputy Principal. Nina Carr was an angel in disguise who changed my life. She taught English, which was my best subject, and took the girls for sport.

'Out of there Carolyn. Come and play hockey.'

She found me hiding in my bush as was my habit during sport time and made me participate. For the first time since we had lived at Macedon, I discovered I was very good at something. I ran like the wind and played hockey extremely well. Nina Carr also corresponded with my mother, who wrote back. They exchanged a number of letters, which I think helped my mother. Nina Carr ended her career as Principal of MacRobertson Girls High School, an elite government school for girls. The position demonstrated that she was the best female teacher in Victoria.

Making my debut

Improvements in my confidence did not help my academic performance. In form 5 (year 11, leaving), I was so pleased with myself I joined a square dance group and 'made my debut' instead of doing homework.

The year came to an abrupt halt when I failed. My mother was extremely cross with me, justifiably so, but for me the exciting year more or less made up for my fail. My mother agreed to let me stay at school for another year, to re-do my Leaving Certificate.

'You have to do all your homework,' she said, 'Or you'll have to leave.'

My emotions and behaviour during my last year at school were the closest match to those I had experienced at Macedon, and that year was best since I had turned ten. I was good at sport and a member of the school teams. I was also successful academically, for the first time since I left Macedon.

I had been a confident, clever, happy-go-lucky child at Macedon, but at Cressy, at the age of ten and a half, I became a lonely, anxious child, with no friends, who cried whenever the headmaster spoke to me.

I was not a natural candidate for an eventual political career, as even into the 1980s I carried snippets of this ingrained low self worth. I used to read the 'Sun Psychologist's' help column' in the paper each Thursday when I was 15. I wanted to be a psychologist. But, of course, I believed I didn't have the brains to attend university. After all, I had failed fifth form the first time.

However, during the last year at school I decided to become a primary teacher, which didn't require matriculation. I applied, and was accepted into Geelong Teachers College for 1955. The future shone ahead.

Twenty five years later I fulfilled the dream I'd held at 15, when I achieved a first class honours degree in psychology, at last proving to myself that I was not the failure I was labelled in that bleak time at Cressy, and that I could achieve anything I liked.

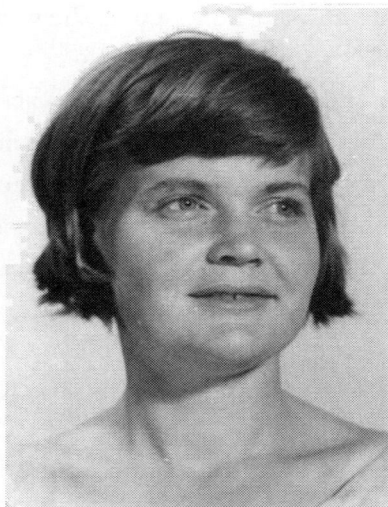

Grown up

CHAPTER 14
CONSEQUENCES

The *Herald Sun* reported my second law-breaking act and the Premier's reaction as follows:

> *Premier Steve Bracks last night ordered one of his MPs to resign from the Labor Party after she was picked up driving while disqualified.*
>
> *Carolyn Hirsh, 67, former chair of the drugs and crime prevention committee, was forbidden to drive after being busted for drink-driving in June.*
>
> *But about noon yesterday, the Upper House member for Silvan Province, who lives in Glen Iris, was pulled over by police and her car was found to be unregistered.*
>
> *Mr Bracks last night demanded her resignation from the party.*
>
> ``*I have late this afternoon spoken to Carolyn Hirsh and told her she must resign from the Labor Party," he said.*

``*(She) should have learned her lesson when her licence was suspended for drink-driving earlier this year.*
``*To be driving a car and failing to display current registration while disqualified are serious matters…*"
"*…There's no room for her in the party. She's been booted out and she will serve as an independent…*"
…A statement from the State Government said Ms Hirsh accepted Mr Bracks' demand.

I did not feel emotionally safe enough to go home that night, and stayed at the home of Anne Eckstein, a friend and colleague, to whom I owe a debt of gratitude for her support. She plied me with wine, and showed me some new clothes she'd bought. I recall later in the night that I moved over in bed to make room for one of her cats to join me, and fell out.

I woke to a media frenzy the next day, with attacks increasing in intensity as newspaper editorials called for my resignation from Parliament, rather than just from the Labor Party.

One commercial radio personality, whom I shall not name, said of media reports,

She apparently told the police officer she was her daughter, and it was her daughter's car. I wonder if that's the daughter that's dead.

'I have to resign from Parliament.' I felt desperate.

'You can't.'

'I need to resign, I can't stay. I can't face this.'

'You have to stay in Parliament,' a friend said. 'It would cause awful damage to the Government. Even worse, you'd cause awful damage to us.'

Us meant friends whom I respected, the group of Outer East marginal seat holders. They were right. If I resigned from Parliament, there would be a by-election for Silvan Province, which the Labor Party would likely lose.

'Remember, the Opposition is running a massive campaign against Eastlink.'

'If you resign, Silvan will be a shoe-in for the Liberals.'

The government had reneged on a promise to build the long awaited Scoresby Freeway and an extension to the Eastern Freeway to meet the Scoresby. Instead, private contractors would build a toll road. The Liberal Party campaign against this policy change was vocal and very successful.

My friends argued that an inevitable Labor loss in a by-election in Silvan Province would be a disaster in the marginal lower house electorates of the Outer East, for Labor's majority in the Legislative Council, and for the Labor Government.

I could not stay, but could not resign.

❖

My daughter, Teresa, rang a psychiatrist I had seen on and off from the time that Vicki's illness had become severe. He arranged for my admission to a psychiatric clinic. He admitted me under a false name, since media outlets were doing all they could to locate me. They hounded my family, and a journalist from a tabloid newspaper even tracked down my brother and sister-in-law.

I spent about two weeks in the clinic. I recall making attractive cards in an occupational therapy group. I heard no radio, saw no television and read no newspapers. While I was there, taking some sort of mind-numbing medication for some days, I concluded firstly, that the healthiest thing I could do for myself was to leave Parliament, and secondly, that I could not do so because of the damage my resignation would do to my Labor colleagues and the Government. I chose to ignore my own feelings, advice of doctors and the wellbeing of my family, and stay on as a Member of Parliament, albeit no longer as a Labor Party Member.

❖

I returned to Parliament, as an Independent Member, sitting in a spot between the opposing parties. This was a further reminder of the 'lost' years of my childhood at lunch times in the playground at Cressy.

The first day back in Parliament was painful. Of course, I was not allowed to attend the usual Tuesday morning lineup of Labor Party meetings — left faction, caucus meeting, and upper house party meeting, where the Bills and strategies for the week ahead were discussed. I did not have to arrive until 2.00 pm when the bells rang for the start of the sitting. I was so lonely. I lost my Parliamentary office, because it was assigned to the Labor Party.

'You can share with Dianne Hadden,' John Lenders told me.

Dianne Hadden was a Member of the Labor Party in the Legislative Council who had resigned from the Party not long before.

I eventually inherited Dianne Hadden's old spot — in a Labor Party office, sharing with former Labor Party colleague and upper house Member, Jenny Mikakos. I was fighting an emotional battle to stay in Parliament, and was hanging onto a degree of sanity by cobweb threads. I think this demonstration of trust by the Leader of the Legislative Council, John Lenders, and President Monica Gould, as well as their decision to place my seat in the Chamber on the Labor Party side, just enabled me to continue.

I managed to retrieve from somewhere and strengthen the brittle shell I had worn from the time of my election, and entered the Chamber clothed in my usual aura of composure. *If I have to stay in Parliament and be an Independent Member, I'll show them I can do it.* I put my name down for a Member's Statement, and made a speech about a school in my electorate of Silvan Province, reproduced from Hansard below.

> *<u>Hon. C. D. HIRSH (Silvan)</u> - Last week I had the pleasure of attending the opening by the Premier of the new school hall at Bayswater Primary School. It was a great event and a great occasion. This year the school is celebrating its 125th anniversary. It started out in 1879 in a wooden building with four rooms - very small rooms - and is now a very well equipped state primary school offering a comprehensive education to local primary students.*
>
> *The hall is state of the art, contributed to by the state Government and by local parents, who do an amazing job. Any member who would like to donate $20 will receive a tile which will be in the grounds with their name on it. That would be very much appreciated by the school, and I am sure it would be a good idea for everyone to look at doing that.*

Even in the last five years the buildings have been modernised, updated and upgraded so that the students now work in a very pleasant environment. There are no more of the old open fires with only those students who got there early getting near the fire; the rooms are comprehensively comfortable as far as temperature goes, and working conditions are excellent.

I also tried to place a Notice of Motion on the Notice Paper about my electorate, but did not consult the Clerk about its wording. My attempt triggered a debate covering two pages of Hansard, about whether the wording of the notice was appropriate.

I was grateful to a many of my Labor Party colleagues for their individual support during this period, and to a number of Members of both the Liberal and National Parties.

❖

The Victorian Parliamentary dining room is an anachronism, resembling the dining room of a boarding school, or the Teachers' College hostel I lived in for two years at age 18. A long table is set for each Party: Labor, Liberal and National. In the 55th Parliament, there was also a small table for the two remaining Independents who had supported a minority Labor Government in 1999, and Dianne Hadden, who had resigned from the Labor Party. As I entered the dining room on my first day as an Independent, a staff member directed me to the small table in the centre of the dining room, where a place had been set for me. I fled.

I almost ran out of the Parliament building, down the imposing front steps and along Bourke Street. I stopped outside a building with a familiar sign that had been providing me with comfort through a form of hypnosis — a poker machine venue. I took to hiding there, engaged in thought-blocking behaviour, during many lunch times, gradually adding to what was to become half of 'the full bogan package' of addiction that I finally acknowledged a few years later. I would leave in time for the bells heralding the commencement of Parliament, and as I walked back up the hill and ascended the steps, I would sheath myself in the brittle shell that enabled me to enter the Legislative Council Chamber.

❖

A court case took place at the Melbourne Magistrate's Court on 15 March, 2005. The Labor Party provided me with support — a solicitor and a barrister to represent me. The Barrister representing me painted a clear picture of my loss and shame, and the Magistrate was quite sympathetic — he applied a three-month licence suspension and a $600 fine. I was quite efficient at donning my armour by this time, and made a statement to the media thronging outside the court. *At last, it's over,* or so I thought.

As the year went on, I slowly redeemed myself with the public and the Labor Party — not with myself though. Even the Premier agreed late in the year to 'allow' me back into the Labor Party. *The Herald-Sun* reported his decision.

A spokeswoman for Mr Bracks, Alison Crosweller, said

yesterday he had forgiven Ms Hirsh.

``*The Premier felt a significant period of time had elapsed since Carolyn Hirsh's resignation and she had undergone a significant public penalty," Ms Crosweller said.*

❖

If only the horror had stopped then.

I was a lot better, and rejoining the Labor Party helped my return to some level of normality. My granddaughter had finished school at the end of 2004 — gaining a brilliant ENTER score of 97.2. I was so proud of her achievement, which she managed despite the erratic nature of her life with me.

My mental state did not improve enough though, and I still neglected to seek appropriate ongoing treatment. I remember making irregular visits to the psychiatrist who had admitted me to the clinic, and I took the antidepressant tablets he prescribed. However, while not addicted to alcohol at that stage, I probably drank enough to negate most of the benefits of the medication. Perhaps this limited treatment helped me limp through life, keeping my armour of normality in place. I was suffering from more than depression, but did not know what. A range of images — flashbacks would accompany the unthinkable thoughts and unbearable emotions that flicked through my mind. I was easily startled, and reacted with psychological distress and a physical panic reaction to the slightest surprise.

Michael Leunig's cartoon in *The Saturday Age* on 25 June 2011 said everything for which I had no words.

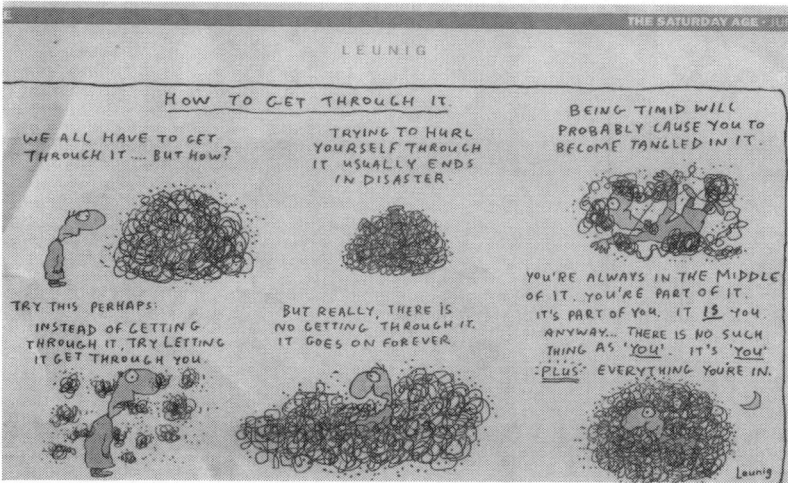

Courtesy of Michael Leunig: The Saturday Age June 25, 2011

To get rid of the mental and emotional intruders which still accompanied me I 'kept busy', blanked out my mind at a poker machine venue, or had another glass of wine. I can now name the elements of my shadowy inner life as horror, grief and guilt, joined by shame and humiliation. Five years later, I was diagnosed as suffering from post-traumatic stress disorder (PTSD), as well as addiction to alcohol and poker machines. PTSD can develop after exposure to an extremely traumatic event that causes a reaction of intense fear, horror or helplessness. The American Psychiatric Association suggests that finding the body of someone who has committed suicide can be a precursor to PTSD.

CHAPTER 15

VICKI'S LIFE — THE PARADOX REVISITED

I didn't believe a member of my family could do such things, but Vicki did.

A calm few months followed the massive tantrum Vicki had thrown on the morning of my mother's funeral in early April 1986. She and Jeff seemed happy as we organised their wedding — Vicki was tranquil and behaved maturely. Her delightful sense of humour was front and centre. They went house hunting and planned for the birth of their baby, due in October. Jeff put a deposit on a house in suburban Ashburton. *It all seemed normal.*

They were married in August 1986 at Kenloch, a wedding reception venue at Olinda in the Dandenong Ranges. By the time of the wedding, Vicki was seven months pregnant, so Teresa helped her exchange the size ten wedding dress she had bought in April for a size sixteen. The wedding was wonderful. Two bridesmaids wore fashionable purple, families and friends attended, and Vicki maintained responsible, adult behaviour.

❖

In the weeks after Jessica's birth, Vicki rang me regularly and tearfully, at work, at home and late at night.

'The baby keeps crying and I don't know what to do.'

'She's just vomited all her feed, she'll starve.'

'She won't suck properly. What will I do?'

I would ask the Whip for leave from Parliament so I could help her with the baby, but I saw nothing abnormal with this need for help from a first-time mother, although Jessica was a placid baby. I didn't see Vicki's stay in a mother-baby unit when Jessica was three weeks old as odd either. Both Vicki and Jeff were exemplary parents during Jessica's babyhood — Vicki bought every book on parenting she could find — and Jessica had a great start to life despite Vicki's anxiety. After a few months, Vicki went back to work, to a well-paid job at Telstra, while Jeff stayed home to care for Jessica.

'After all,' Vicki said, 'I earn a lot more than Jeff.'

Despite flickers of misgiving, I kept silent, hoping that marriage and motherhood had finally launched Vicki into maturity.

Her composure lasted until Jessica was about nine months old. It was shattered by a holiday in Fiji, *my holiday in hell*. The events that brought about this holiday demonstrate my complicity — at some level — in Vicki's irresponsible and impulsive behaviour, because I had difficulty saying 'no' to her, even when her requests became demands that I considered unreasonable.

How did I let it happen? I had taken my youngest daughter, Belinda on a couple of interstate train trips — because I was a widow, I was able to list her as my partner for parliamentary functions and visits. Vicki said she needed a break and wanted me to take her interstate too. I said I'd try to organise it, but she called a few days later, excitedly waving tickets.

'I've booked a week in Fiji for both of us. I said you'd drop a cheque in at lunch time.'

'You've what?' I was flabbergasted.

'It's a five star resort, and it's a great special.'

'That's not what we agreed to,' I said.

'Yes, but it's a fantastic bargain, and I need a break. I'm exhausted.'

I ended up paying for the Fiji package, and discovered we were not travelling together. I tried to change the dates, but it was locked in. No changes, no refund.

Vicki left a few days before me, and came home a few days earlier. When I arrived in Fiji, I found Vicki ensconced in our twin share room with a man she had met on the plane — she'd booked me into a single room. She largely ignored me for the four days our stay overlapped. How could she behave so immorally? How had I let her manipulate me into this situation? Why was I so weak? I wasn't weak with anyone else.

❖

Vicki left her husband and daughter when Jessica was three, and moved in with Michael, a work colleague with whom she'd been having an affair. I was furious with her, partly because she left Jeff, but mainly because she left Jessica, an act I could not comprehend. She visited Jessica often, but at irregular times, usually unannounced, and she still kept many of her things at 'home'.

A few months after Vicki moved in, Michael left Australia for three years to undertake a PhD at Cambridge University, so Vicki left her lucrative job and used the payout to follow Michael overseas. She went twice, for about two months each time. I was dismayed that Jessica did not see her mother for such long periods. She missed her a lot, and would often cry and ask, 'Why doesn't Mummy come to see me anymore?'

Between her overseas visits, Vicki stayed in Michael's house. I didn't see a great deal of her. I think she was avoiding me because of my disapproval of her behaviour. *Would I have been supportive if I'd known she had a mental illness?* I found out months later that he rang her a few hours after she arrived back from her second visit to Cambridge and called off the relationship.

Jessica had been pining for her mother, so the morning after Vicki came home, Jeff took Jessica to see her. I knew Jeff had arranged this visit, as I'd been speaking to him and to Vicki on the phone.

My phone rang. It was Jeff.

'I'm at Vicki's and she's in bed and I can't wake her. Jessie's with me.'

'Call an ambulance.'

I arrived as paramedics slid a stretcher with Vicki, still unconscious, into the ambulance and took her to the Alfred Hospital. She had taken an overdose of something. I can't remember what.

That was the first episode of Vicki's drug abuse that I knew about, and the real start of hers and my nightmare. *I later understood that hers had started a long time before that.*

❖

When Jessica was about six years old, Jeff sold the family home and he and Jessica moved in with Sandra*, a single parent with one son a couple of years younger than Jessica. They'd met at the beach the previous summer. This created problems for Vicki, who was no longer able to see Jessica whenever she chose. A court order awarded Vicki and Jeff joint custody, with Jeff to retain day-to-day care of Jessica. The court formalised Vicki's access, by ruling that Jessica stay with her mother every other weekend. The order angered Vicki and she developed a strong hatred for Sandra.

Meanwhile Kevin appeared in Vicki's life, and she moved in with him. He was a delightful person, as were most of Vicki's partners. I trusted him with Jessica, who liked him. In return, he was good to Jessica and loved Vicki dearly.

However, Vicki's general demeanour deteriorated. She took drug overdoses and began self-mutilating. Kevin would ring me from time to time in a panic to tell me that Vicki was behaving strangely, had gone to hospital by ambulance following an overdose, or had cut herself.

Sometimes when I went to their flat I would find Vicki disoriented and apparently in a psychotic state. I realised years later that her bizarre behaviour during this period was more likely to be related to drug or alcohol abuse than psychosis.

She also took to ringing my daughter Teresa and me at home or work, declaring that she was going to kill herself or that she had already taken an overdose. This was often just prior to an access weekend with Jessica, and the call was to tell one or

---

* Not her real name

another of us that we needed to care for Jessica.

She was admitted to a private psychiatric hospital, her first admission of many, where she stayed two or three weeks. During this time, her psychiatrist refused to continue treating her when she cut herself after agreeing not to.

I requested a meeting with him.

'What is wrong with her?' I asked. 'Does she have schizophrenia or bi-polar disorder?'

'No,' he replied. 'She has a severe borderline personality disorder.' (BPD).

I had never heard of this illness, so I spent hours in the biomedical library at Monash University, reading everything I could find about it — there was no *Google* in those times. I was relieved to find out what was wrong with Vicki, and I had no doubt that the diagnosis was correct. The more I read, the more sense Vicki's periodic bizarre behaviour made.

People with this illness are hard to live with, and Vicki showed everyone in her world how true this is. I learned more about it. I read and asked experts, and found that sufferers of BPD live in an immature psychological world, in which they experience deep emptiness, extreme anxiety and a strong fear of abandonment. They try to shield themselves from these feelings through impulsive behaviour and various forms of self-harm. They experience themselves and others in their world as one thing or another, black and white, good or bad, as a toddler does. They appear not be able to experience or see subtle nuances of emotions and relationships that normally develop with maturity. This 'black and white' thinking creates problems enough, but the intensity of the emotions they experience makes matters worse. They seem to have little ability to regulate these dramatic emotional swings. As well, their perceptions of themselves, others and situations around them can shift from one position to another on a daily or even hourly basis.

I learned that the onset of BPD is usually during late adolescence, that the illness is difficult to treat, and that alcohol and drug dependence are common among sufferers. In some ways, I was relieved to have a label to explain Vicki's behaviour, but in other ways, I was more distressed. I am convinced that the illness was related to her father's sudden death a week before she turned 13 and a lack of support after his death. *More complicity on my part.*

❖

Over the next few years, Vicki's 'dialectic' behaviour pattern continued. She alternated between months of reasonably 'normal' behaviour and periods when she would behave like a small child. She broke off the relationship with Kevin, which devastated him. She changed boyfriends a couple more times, changed psychiatrists a few times, moved house a few times, took overdoses and engaged in self-mutilating behaviour. She took several trips overseas, which were always problematic. She seemed unable to cope with the stress of travelling. For example, she went to London, but rang me late on the night she left, from a hotel room in Bangkok, weeping. Her call terrified me.

'Mum, I'm at a hotel in Bangkok. The plane's delayed. There are insects crawling all over my pillow and through my hair.'

'Call the management,' I said. 'Tell them what's going on and ask them to put you in another room.' 'Then have a hot shower and wash your hair.'

Half an hour later, she rang again hysterical.

'This room is worse. They're crawling all over the bed.'

I hung up and rang the hotel manager.

'There's nothing on her bed,' he said. 'She's imagining it.'

I asked him to call a doctor, and for the doctor to ring me.

'I have given her an injection and she has gone to sleep,' the doctor said. 'Someone will wake her in time for the plane tomorrow. Does she take medication?' Does she have a mental illness?' He asked.

I did not reply.

I didn't hear from Vicki in the morning, but she rang from London hours later, sounding normal.

'I got here safely,' she said.

'Whatever happened to you in Bangkok?' I asked.

'I had a terrible migraine and the hotel doctor gave me something to help me sleep.'

She appeared not to remember her frantic calls to me, or her hallucinations about insects.

The rest of her London trip and the direct flight home were without incident. And she brought home presents for Jessica and six or so rolls of photos.

❖

Through the 1990s Vicki worked most of the time — in very good jobs. She was intelligent and competent, but always resigned after a year or two, or her employer sacked her as her relationships with staff and colleagues deteriorated.

She took to suffering from a series of physical ailments and increasingly visited hospital casualty departments and made late night calls to 24-hour locum services. She complained often of migraines and abdominal pain, so severe that she would need strong pain relief. As well, she underwent a number of surgical procedures over a couple of years, some of which I was aware of, others, not until later. She had knee surgery, laparoscopic investigations, removal of her gallbladder, hemorrhoids, a facelift, breast implants, two pregnancy terminations, reversal of the breast implants, treatment for kidney stones, repairs to self-inflicted cuts, plastic surgery on the scars left by self-inflicted cuts, and a surgical investigation of hip pain. I understood later that the common factor in all this was pethidine, which helped to relieve her inner agony.

❖

Vicki was discharged from a psychiatric clinic, homeless, penniless and unemployed, so I bought a small house for her to live in for the time being. It was only a few streets from me and I hoped it would give her stability to enable her to get a job and have Jessica visit. I did not insist on rent, since she was not working. However, shortly after she moved in I discovered she was renovating the kitchen, having the house painted and had acquired a new boyfriend, Paul, who'd moved in. He didn't pay rent either, despite the fact that he had a job.

After a few months, they both moved out, without notice, and left me with a freshly painted house, a renovated kitchen and bill for $10,000. *How had I allowed this to happen?*

Vicki and Paul moved to his flat. She stayed there for a couple of months. I neither liked nor trusted Paul, and I was not keen on Jessica being there. However the relationship did not last.

Vicki rang me at work one evening. My difficulty was that

I was in Canberra.

'I have a knife. I've cut my arm and I'm going to stab myself in the chest.'

She was sobbing and distraught, but I eventually found out what had caused the crisis.

'Paul has told me to get out. I have to kill myself.'

I rang the police, who broke in when she wouldn't answer the door, removed the knife, called an ambulance, and on my instructions took her to the psychiatric hospital she had been in the previous time. I didn't leave work to rush back to Melbourne. *Nothing I did helped.*

When she was due to be discharged, she rang me.

'Can I move back into the house?'

'No, I've rented it out, and I'm still paying your last lot of bills.'

This was one of the first times I said 'no' to Vicki. It was hard.

'You're cruel and totally neglectful,' Vicki replied. 'I'm homeless, and I can't have Jessica with me if I'm in emergency accommodation.' She knew how much I wanted Jessica to be with her mother.

Perhaps this refusal was a good thing for Vicki. Perhaps it was the cruelest action I could have taken. However, she was in the care of a fine psychiatrist, and she improved. She gained an excellent job with Nortel, one of the bourgeoning multinational telecommunications companies encouraged by the Howard Government to compete with Telstra. She established a new relationship with another seemingly pleasant man, Peter. They became engaged early in the liaison, which seemed to give Vicki a sense of security — it helped dissipate the emptiness and fear of abandonment that haunted her.

They put a deposit on a house in suburban Ashburton, and

Vicki undertook the legal process of becoming Jessica's primary carer, which both she and Jessica wanted a lot. I supported her actions since she seemed to have recovered, was holding down a well-paid job, and was in a stable relationship with a man who appeared likable and trustworthy.

So after six years Jessica came back to live with her mother. Vicki was at the helm of a 'normal' family life. She acquired two little white fluffy dogs, Doogle and Pippi, who were doted on by the whole family. Vicki enrolled Jessica at Korowa Anglican Girls' Grammar School, to start year seven in 1999. Life was good.

CHAPTER 16

...AND HER DEATH

The good life didn't last.

I was helping Vicki a couple of evenings a week by picking Jessica up from school, preparing the evening meal and generally assisting with domestic tasks. Jessica and I had a great time.

The downward spiral started when Vicki left Nortel after about a year and a half — or perhaps she was sacked. She didn't seem upset. Two weeks later she rang me.

'Mum I'm so excited. I've been appointed National Marketing Manager of Plestel. It's a new telecommunications company. It's going worldwide.'

Plestel had actually been a part of Telstra that had been sold off, again courtesy of the Howard government's attitude towards publicly owned monopolies. But for Vicki, the new job was wonderful — with a lucrative salary and a car.

One evening when I was at Vicki's with Jessica, Vicki had

not arrived home by 8.00 pm. I was frantic. The phone rang. I grabbed it. It was a local police station.

'Are you Ms. Carolyn Hirsh?'

'Yes,' I replied. 'What's happened?'

'We have your daughter, Victoria Hirsh here. She has been involved in a car accident and is unable to drive. Can someone pick her up please?'

Vicki had been involved in a collision with another car, while under the influence of pethidine and alcohol. She had not been watching the road because she had been drinking wine from a bottle as she drove. No one was hurt, for which I was grateful, but Vicki's company car was a write-off, and she received a fine. Of course, the insurance company would not cover the cost of the car —Vicki was personally liable.

Her long period of emotional stability began to fray after the car smash, and she changed psychiatrists, which was detrimental for her. Her new psychiatrist was an older woman who knew nothing of borderline personality disorder, and to whom Vicki would lie with impunity.

By late 1999 we were all back on the mental illness merry-go-round, exacerbated by Vicki's gradually acquired addiction to pethidine, which had become full-blown by this time. She complained to her psychiatrist of regular severe 'migraines' which only pethidine could relieve. I tried to arrange a meeting with the psychiatrist to inform her of Vicki's actual illness, that she didn't suffer migraines, and that she had developed an addiction to pethidine.

'I can't discuss a patient,' the psychiatrist told me firmly.

'But she's pulling the wool over your eyes,' I said.

She refused to listen or speak to me, and Vicki refused to allow me to attend a joint session with her. Psychiatrists can sometimes do more harm than good.

Vicki was dismissed from her job at this time, and her alcohol and drug use intensified. She began self-mutilating again, even in front of Jessica. Jessica rang me more than once from a hospital emergency department, asking me to pick her up, as the ambulance crew wouldn't leave her at home on her own when they had to take Vicki to hospital after she had overdosed or cut herself.

Before Christmas 1999, she cut herself so badly — through blood vessels, tendons and nerves — that she needed plastic surgery and weeks with her arm in plaster. Early in 2000 she was admitted to the intensive care section of another psychiatric hospital, where she spent three weeks because she was threatening suicide. She was detoxified from all the drugs in her system, but as soon as she was allowed onto an open ward, she began using pethidine and alcohol again.

Soon after her discharge, she began having trouble getting hold of pethidine — she had been 'doctor shopping' a lot. Apparently she had been found out and 'flagged' in some way. Another new psychiatrist admitted her to the drug and alcohol section of a suburban psychiatric hospital instead of the general section she had always gone in the past. Here, another patient in the drug and alcohol section taught her how to obtain and use to heroin. To me, when I found out, it was as if the sky had fallen in. I think now it was probably a lot like that for Vicki too.

During the rest of 2000 Jessica spent more than half the time with me, as Vicki tried to get off the heroin, but could not. She went back to hospital a few times, undertook the 'methadone' heroin substitution program, drank a lot of alcohol, took prescription drugs and overdosed a few times. A number of incidents compromised Jessica's safety, so I decided Jessica needed to stay with me until Vicki managed to give up drugs and alcohol.

There was a delightful interlude in this 'annus horribilus', in September when I took Jessica to week one of the Sydney Olympics — a trip I had planned 18 months earlier. We forgot our problems and had a ball.

❖

I decided I had to move. Jeff lived in Glen Iris, and Vicki nearby in Ashburton. I wanted to keep Jessica at her school in Glen Iris, and near both her parents, so I sold up and bought a unit in Glen Iris. We moved on 5 March 2001.

Vicki's condition continued to deteriorate. I found it impossible to tell which aspects of her behaviour were drug and alcohol related, and which were part of her illness. She was unemployed and her partner left her in January 2001. She was angry with me and in despair with herself. I could see nothing of the clever, funny and beautiful person who had once existed.

On Friday 23 March 2001, I came home from work about 5.00 pm and found a fat envelope in the letterbox, addressed to me in Vicki's handwriting. It was a four-page suicide letter. I panicked, drove to her place — empty, and rang the hospital and her current psychiatrist.

'I saw her at four o'clock,' the psychiatrist said. 'She seemed fine. She has a job and is due to start on Monday.'

I was reassured, but still did not know where she was. At 8.00 pm the phone rang. It was the Accident and Emergency department at Box Hill Hospital.

'Victoria took a serious overdose of heroin and was brought

here by ambulance. She has had narcan and is now stable.'

'She left me a long suicide letter. Please look after her,' I said. I realised Vicki had made a serious suicide attempt this time, and probably would have died had the heroin not been cut to such a weak mix, due to a shortage at the time.

'We're keeping her in overnight and she will have a psychiatric assessment in the morning. She doesn't want you to come to the hospital.'

I felt relieved that Vicki was safe, and hoped that perhaps this clinic might be able to help her.

I could not sleep and was still up at midnight when the phone rang again. It was Vicki. She sounded normal.

'I discharged myself. It's a disgusting place.'

'What about that letter?'

'I did mean to kill myself, but it didn't work, so when I woke up I called an ambulance to take me to hospital. I'll see my psychiatrist in the morning. I'm alright now Mum. I won't do it again'

The next day, Saturday, Vicki did see her psychiatrist and had lunch with a friend. I had a few phone conversations with her and she seemed stable.

On the Sunday morning — 25 March, I rang her again. She was despondent.

'I have no food and no money.'

'Come around here and I'll make some soup for lunch.' She lived a ten minute drive away.

'No,' she said. 'I don't feel well enough to drive.'

'Then I'll make a pot of shank and barley soup with vegetables and bring it around when it's cooked,' I said. Shank and barley soup is my panacea for all ills.

'I suppose you can. Don't tell Jessica I'm not well.'

'She's going to the pictures with Shelley Robinson* and her family later. Do you want me to wait and come after they've left?' I was trying so hard not to upset her.

'Yes, that's the best,' she replied.

'What will you do for the next few hours?' I asked. I felt helpless.

'I'll read.'

I rang her again an hour later.

'The soup's cooking. Are you alright? *Inane question.*

'You don't need to come now,' she said. 'I'm reading.'

I rang again an hour later, but Vicki did not answer. I got her voice message. *Such a normal voice.*

'Hello this is Victoria. I'm not available now, but please leave a message and your number and I'll call you back as soon as I can.'

I tried her phone twice more, still her voicemail.

I felt something was wrong, but told myself she was alright. *A friend's called in and they've gone to lunch. The sun is out, she's decided to do some gardening.*

I left the phone alone for another hour and made sandwiches for Jessica and myself at lunchtime. I remember they were cheese and tomato sandwiches. I ate half a sandwich, and rang Vicki again. The sandwich turned into a rock in my stomach. Vicki's message had gone. Her voice on the answering machine had disappeared. A computerised male voice with an American accent said:

'No one is available to take your call. Please leave a message after the tone.'

I rang a few more times, thinking Vicki might answer, but she didn't. I began to feel frightened again. *Why had she deleted*

---

* Not her real name

her phone message?

As soon as Jessica left with the Robinsons, I put the soup in the car and set off for Vicki's, my hands sweaty, trembling on the steering wheel as I drove. I parked carefully outside her house, lining the car wheels neatly alongside the gutter.

Pippi and Doogle, Vicki's two dogs, were in the front garden instead of the back where they should have been. The gate to the backyard was open. *This is weird.* I looked in Vicki's bedroom window at the front. *No. The bed's empty.* I rushed to the lounge room window. I could see the empty couch. Relief flooded through me. *She's all right, she's gone out.*

I looked around for her car — there it was, parked near the fence next to the garage, but the garage door was half-open. I walked over and peered around the door into the half dark. There were some clothes hanging from the steel rafter.

I looked more closely. It was not just clothes. Her head was twisted forward, face blue. One shoe was missing from a dangling foot, which was bent at right angles to the other. Her hands hung still. I grabbed a hand. It was as cold as ice.

❖

There are so many questions that I will never answer. Would Vicki have committed suicide if her father had not died? What effect did my neglect of her afterwards have? What if she'd been able to say goodbye to him? What if she'd been allowed to attend his funeral? What if I'd been firmer with her as a teenager and a young adult? What if I'd stopped her going to England when she was 18?

These questions haunted me for ten years after Vicki's death, along with the big one. Was it my fault? The answer following the question was always, 'Yes.'

My memories of the ten years following Vicki's suicide, including four years in Parliament, exist in a fog. Sometimes it drifts aside and I am able to access a movie of one or another event, but layers of shame or guilt or anger or despair still wrap around many memories.

Just one episode early in my last year of Parliament is swathed in a sense of achievement and satisfaction. I decided I had to try to make amends for my behaviour, to attempt to do something useful.

CHAPTER 17
MAKING AMENDS

I was grateful I'd been allowed back in the Labor Party late in 2005. My seat in the House had been moved again, to acknowledge my re-entry, to the back row on the Government side.

'You may as well stay in the same office,' John Lenders, upper house leader, said, so I'd kept my spot in the shared office with Jenny Mikakos. I went back to left faction meetings and caucus meetings, although I was quieter than I'd been before my 'troubles', and had to be careful not to burst into tears in front of anyone. The main difficulty with being back in the Labor Party was the need to keep my mask of normality in place for much longer periods. I joined a Joint Parliamentary Committee — not the Drugs and Crime Prevention Committee that I'd chaired previously. Don Nardella, the Member for Melton, chaired the Outer Suburban and Infrastructure Committee, and he welcomed me as a member. I attended committee meetings, but had trouble concentrating on the policy work under investigation, because most of the time I had to focus on keeping a smile on my made-up face. *Get over your own worries. Stop thinking about yourself. Do something for someone else. Get involved with policy you really care about.*

So I did.

During the four years of my term in Parliament, a crucial issue had simmered along. Coming to a boil every now and then, it had been on my radar since the election in 2002. It was so important to me that its escalation in early 2006 was sufficient to drag me from my morass of shame and despair. The issue of abortion was front and centre in the media, discussed publicly and loudly.

Until October 2008, abortion was prohibited in Victoria under sections 65 and 66 of the Crimes Act. The law was based on S58 of the UK *Offences Against the Persons Act, 1861* with penalties ranging from 10 to 14 years jail for anyone convicted of unlawfully using an instrument, drug, or other noxious thing with intent to procure a miscarriage on a woman.

❖

My first involvement with abortion was in 1959 when my friend who taught in a country school, and boarded in the country town, became pregnant to a local grazier's son. He gave her some money and the address of an abortion clinic in Melbourne. She stayed with my new husband and me while she had the abortion.

There were two types of abortions available, both illegal. If the pregnant woman had little money, she could go to a backyard abortionist, usually not a doctor. They were dangerous procedures and there was a ward at the Women's Hospital where many of these women ended up with infections and haemorrhaging. Some died. If a woman had £500, she could have an abortion done by a qualified doctor, in sterile conditions. My friend had the money so she booked into the latter service. It was an unpleasant experience for her, just the same. She had to sign a waiver, absolving the doctor of responsibility if anything went wrong.

In the late 1960s, Dr Bertram Wainer brought a common practice to the attention of the public. A group of doctors who performed illegal abortions was paying corrupt police — they were buying protection from prosecution. The corrupt police officers went to jail. Bertram Wainer opened the first affordable abortion clinic, in East Melbourne, and dared the police to prosecute him. However, they did not.

In 1969, Justice Menhennitt ruled in the Supreme Court in Victoria that an abortion was lawful if there was serious danger to the life or physical or mental health of the mother without it. Although abortion remained in the Crimes Act, this case law sent backyard abortionists and corrupt police packing, and eventually abortions became available in most public hospitals.

This situation prevailed when I was in Parliament between 1985 and 1992. Along with the other pro-choice women in Parliament, I took an attitude of, *it seems to be working, leave it alone.*

The situation changed in the twenty-first century. One issue that brought abortion back into the public arena was the RU486 (mifepristone) debate in the Federal Parliament, which stirred up the topic and brought the 'Right to Life' lobby out in force. RU486 is a drug that can bring about an abortion in a woman who is under nine weeks pregnant. A medical abortion using mifepristone is safer than the usual surgical abortion, easier for women, particularly in regional Australia to access, and less expensive.

The Prime Minister at the time, John Howard, had done a deal with Senator Brian Harradine in order to secure his vote. Senator Harradine was a rabid anti-abortionist, so John Howard offered to make RU486 available only with the approval of the Minister for Health and Ageing, rather than the Therapeutic Goods Administration, (TGA), who should have controlled it. This political fix made the drug generally unavailable to women.

A cross-party group of women, Senators Lyn Allison of the Democrats and Fiona Nash of The Nationals, Judith Troeth of the Liberal Party and Claire Moore of the Australian Labor Party introduced a Private Members Bill into the Federal Parliament. Its purpose was to return control of RU486 to the TGA, and it passed, despite a ferocious campaign by the 'Right to Life'.

❖

I made my first statement in the Victorian Parliament about abortion on 10 November 2004, while I was serving as an independent, and was not answerable to my Party. It was based on the Right to Life rumblings in Canberra and Victoria. I reproduce it below.

Over the last couple of weeks a group of men in Canberra
have opened up a debate on abortion, and its supposed rights

and wrongs. So far few women have been heard in this latest debate...

...I strongly believe it is time for the discussion to be taken over by women. I grew up in Victoria where abortion was illegal and dangerous, undertaken clandestinely at a very high cost, payable in cash -- and sometimes with the life of the woman. In 1969 in Victoria this situation changed when Justice Menhennit directed that it was legal to terminate a pregnancy if it was to protect the woman's life or health from dangers other than the normal dangers of pregnancy.

This common-law precedent made legal access to abortion possible in Victoria. However, abortion is still in the Crimes Act in Victoria -- sections 65 and 66 -- a relic from British law passed in 1862. These sections in the Victorian statutes should be repealed, and the abortion debate should change its focus from the so-called moral issues to whether a woman's decision to undertake the medical procedure of abortion should have anything to do with government at all.

I made another statement the day before the vote on RU486 took place in Canberra, supporting the position of the women MPs who sponsored the Bill. I was back in the Labor Party by this time, but no one seemed concerned about me talking about abortion.

Today I want to express the strong hope that federal members of Parliament will vote to support the lifting of the ban on mifepristone, which is also known as RU486. Mifepristone is used to procure medical abortions for women. Through extensive clinical trials and the drug's use in Europe and the United States of America mifepristone has been shown to be equally as safe as a surgical abortion and is often preferred by women.

The ban in Australia was negotiated on political and ideological grounds between John Howard and Brian Harradine. That had nothing to do with women's medical needs. To have medical matters used by politicians and ideologues is unethical.

It is appalling generally that matters concerning women and their health, whether or not the health issue is to do with pregnancy, is bandied around as a political football by a bunch of people, many of whom are men and have no business in interfering with women's health matters. I urge federal politicians to support the lifting of that ban in Australia so that women will have proper choices when making medical decisions about their own health and their own future. We should not be interfering in matters that concern women and their doctors.

The Bill passed the Federal Parliament early in 2006, and although mifepristone can still be hard to get, decisions about its use are out of political hands.

I made another speech congratulating the Bill's sponsors, reproduced below.

Hon. C. D. HIRSH (Silvan) -- I rise today to congratulate

*Senators Lyn Allison of the Democrats, Fiona Nash of The
Nationals, Judith Troeth of the Liberal Party and Claire
Moore of the Australian Labor Party for sponsoring the bill
to remove the abortion drug RU486, mifepristone, from
the jurisdiction of the federal health minister to that of the
Therapeutic Goods Administration, which is far better
qualified to decide on its safety and efficacy for Australians.*

*I also congratulate the Australian Parliament on passing
the bill. However, here in Victoria we still have unfinished
business. While abortion is legal under common law due to
Justice Menhennit's ruling in 1969, there is still an anomaly
in Victoria, with abortion still being included in sections
10, 64 and 65 of the Crimes Act. It is time for Victoria
to remove this anomaly and to ensure that Victorian women
have access to safe, medically performed abortion.*

❖

The second issue that brought the abortion debate to public
notice and created difficulties for women seeking abortions was
a Victorian one, although a Federal Senator created the public
mischief.

In 2000, a woman whose fetus had been diagnosed with
achondroplasia — a form of dwarfism that cannot be diagnosed
before 24 weeks gestation — arrived at a major public hospital.
She was 31 weeks pregnant and acutely suicidal. Mental health
professionals believed she would kill herself rather than have the
baby she was carrying, so an abortion was performed.

The hospital held a meeting to discuss the ethics of the issue, which led to a great deal of unpleasantness among hospital staff. The hospital's Chief Executive Officer reported the case to the state coroner, and the federal politician, who had somehow acquired detailed information about the case, took it to the media. Eventually a police investigation concluded that the actions of the medical staff were lawful in the circumstances.

However the right to life lobby, with the federal politician at the helm, used the unpleasant nature of late term abortion to publicise the issue of the statutory illegality of abortion. This was despite the fact that less than 1 percent of all abortions are late term, that is, over 20 weeks. Most late term abortions take place because of serious fetal abnormality that cannot be diagnosed early.

❖

I decided I could make amends for my appalling behaviour as a public figure by introducing a Private Members' Bill into the Legislative Council that would remove abortion from the Crimes Act in Victoria. Because it was an election year and neither the Government nor the marginal seat holders wanted the issue of abortion around their electorates, I decided that once the Bill was tabled, I would move that it be sent to the Law Reform Commission for investigation and recommendations. That way the issue would disappear during the election period, but there would be a Bill ready to be passed straight after the election due in November 2006.

I was not sure how to develop a Bill for Parliament as I had not been in Cabinet, and I didn't want to signal my intentions too widely. I felt a Bill that had passed the Australian Capital Territory

(ACT) Parliament could form the basis of a Bill for Victoria. I consulted the Clerks of the Legislative Council, who initially said that Parliamentary Counsel would draft a bill. However, they refused. I spent a long time reading legislation from all over the world, speaking with erudite people, and eventually drafted a Bill that seemed to fit the Victorian position. The Bill repealed sections 65 and 66 in the Crimes Act, where the clauses had sat for 150 years alongside incest, murder and other criminal activities, and addressed other necessary legal matters. I had private discussions with Legislative Council members from all sides — I think my time as an Independent MP had helped me get to know Members in other parties. There were enough numbers in the Legislative Council to gain leave to table the Bill and vote in favour of sending it to the Law Reform Commission.

On the evening before I intended tabling the Bill I spoke to a pro-choice *Age* journalist, Farrah Tomazin, and told her what my intentions were. I felt that if the story ran the next day it would be harder for anyone to stifle me. But I did not realise the length of the tentacles of the Premier's media adviser Sharon McCrohan. She found out what I intended and that an article would appear in *The Age* the next morning. The Premier rang me that evening and ordered me to cancel any idea I had about Abortion Law reform.

Below is part of an article that Farrah Tomazin wrote seven months later just before the election, about the control the Premier exercised over his fellow Cabinet ministers and backbenchers.

Labor came to office vowing it would be a transparent
government, so why do accusations of secrecy and news

management persist?

Seven months ago, state Labor backbencher Carolyn Hirsh decided to do something bold. A long-time advocate of abortion law reform, Hirsh began talking to colleagues about the prospect of introducing a private members' bill to decriminalise abortion in Victoria.

It was a risky idea. Like any member of the Bracks Government, she knew the rules: sing from the Premier's songbook or do not sing at all. And stay away from controversy.

But the retiring member for Silvan wanted to leave parliament with a legacy of removing abortion from the Crimes Act, a longstanding ALP policy, and she agreed to speak to this newspaper about her plans.

What happened next says a lot about the spin and damage control that underpins the Bracks Government.

It wasn't long before Bracks' media director, Sharon McCrohan, found out that Hirsh had been talking to the media. That evening, McCrohan was on the phone to Hirsh, asking her to retract her comments. At the same time, Bracks' press secretary, Alison Crosweller, rang wanting to know "what angle" was being taken and on what page the story was running. Soon, Bracks was also on the phone to Hirsh. About 10.15pm - after the story had gone to press - Hirsh finally called The Age.

"I'm sorry, I have to make a statement," Hirsh said. "My statement is that the decriminalisation of abortion is an issue I feel very strongly about. However, I have no plans to move in a unilateral way to bring a bill into parliament."

At the direction of the Premier's media unit, Hirsh put out a press release the next morning backing away from the story. The unwanted controversy for Bracks in the lead-up to the November 25 election was effectively killed.

By Farrah Tomazin, 28/10/2006. The Age

❖

Nothing happened about decriminalisation of abortion for the first seven months of the new government until July 2007, until Candy Broad introduced a Private Members' Bill to decriminalise abortion. I was in the gallery, very emotional; Peter Ker from *The Age* wrote the following article.

Carolyn Hirsh wore a red blouse and matching red coat that blended with the red interior of Victoria's Legislative Council.

Yet as Candy Broad rose to introduce her private member's bill yesterday, Ms Hirsh was the most conspicuous person in the room.

Sitting just metres away from Ms Broad in the public gallery, Ms Hirsh clutched her hands as the notice was read.

Upon completion of the short statement, she smiled and was soon fighting back tears.

Just 16 months ago, she had planned to introduce a private member's bill to decriminalise abortion in Victoria, before controversially recanting, under pressure from Steve Bracks in pre-election mode.

Soon afterwards, her political career was over, punctuated by a second drink-driving offence. But there was no dwelling on past disappointments yesterday.

She stood in the chamber and turned to the gallery above, blowing kisses to supporters of her long fight to decriminalise abortion in Victoria.

Within seconds she was gone from the chamber. Outside she hugged and thanked Ms Broad for her courage, before telling reporters she was always hopeful of seeing this day.

"My reaction is one of great excitement and I congratulate Candy Broad... it will be so good for the women of Victoria, and I do urge all members to support the bill," she said.

Peter Ker, 18/07/2007, The Age

Candy went further than I had and presented the second reading speech for a Bill to decriminalise abortion on 19 July 2007. The debate was adjourned until the following week but other events overtook it.

On 27 July 2007 Steve Bracks announced his resignation as Premier and from Parliament, and on August 20, the new Premier, John Brumby announced that the government would decriminalise abortion.

Premier John Brumby has moved to decriminalise abortion, promising to seek advice from the Victorian Law Reform Commission and allow MPs a conscience vote on changes to the law.

"For nearly 40 years the laws relating to abortion have operated in an uncertain legal environment," Mr Brumby said.

Abortion has remained an offence in the Crimes Act, despite a 1969 Supreme Court decision which set out the circumstances in which an abortion was lawful.

"This means that our existing laws are out of step with community sentiment and current clinical practice," Mr Brumby said.

Candy Broad withdrew her Bill from the Parliament the following day.

On 19 August 2008 Maxine Morand, Minister for Women's Affairs, introduced the Abortion Law Reform Bill and presented the second reading. The debate was adjourned until Tuesday 9 September when 62 speakers participated in the second reading debate. The vote for the second reading was 47 in favour of the Bill and 35 against. There was a long committee stage, and the final vote on the Bill was 49 in favour and 32 against.

I was so happy to see the Bill pass and along with most Victorians, I was grateful to Premier John Brumby and Maxine Morand in particular, and those members who voted for the Bill, as they finally removed abortion from the Crimes Act in Victoria.

I had attempted to make some amends to the women of Victoria for my illegal behaviour, but had failed, although my actions may have influenced the eventual success of the legislation. However doing something worthwhile in the service of my values had been good for me. I was still not well in the months I developed the Bill and prepared to table it, but I was better than I had been. After I backed down, unwillingly following the Premier's orders, hopelessness and worthlessness flooded back, and I buried them once more in alcohol and the hypnosis of poker machines.

CHAPTER 18
THIRD STRIKE

I had not thought much about the insidious nature of addiction for some years. Vicki had become addicted to pethidine, then heroin, which ended up killing her, but I did not note any parallels that existed with my own behaviour. Perhaps I should have. With hindsight, it seems that during the years after Vicki's death I mirrored her appalling behaviour with my own. There are similarities. I may have wanted to punish myself, or show Vicki that I could behave as badly as she could.

My father had been an alcoholic and a heavy smoker. He died of a heart attack at age 64. I had been addicted to cigarettes from the age of 18 until I finally quit on 26 August 1983, at the age of 46, on my third serious try. I will never forget how difficult it was to give up smoking.

Addictions are powerful drivers of behaviour and very difficult to recover from. I should have taken notice of my changing behaviour during the first half of 2006 as two addictions — to poker machines and alcohol — began their manipulations of my brain receptors. There were some signs. On the days I was in Parliament, I would get a mental 'itch' around 5.00 pm each afternoon. I would want a glass of wine, and because it was easily available I would head off to the bar and have one, then one with dinner and likely another one or two. I no longer had problems about driving home from Parliament, since I had moved from Glen Iris to Ferntree Gully at the end of 2005. I was living far enough from the city to be eligible for an overnight allowance, so during sitting weeks I stayed overnight across the road from Parliament at the Windsor Hotel.

I had not indulged in regular drinking during my first two Parliamentary terms in the 80s and early 90s. Drinking had been an occasional social activity, but now I found myself looking forward to 5 o'clock so I could have my first glass of wine for the day — I never drank before five o'clock in the afternoon and considered therefore that I was not an alcoholic. After all, my father had his first bottle of beer when he got up in the morning. That was my view of an alcoholic. I should have taken notice of the 'itch', the desire, the need.

I did notice the second 'itch' that was assailing me. It worried me. I no longer bothered with poker machines while Parliament was sitting, but during non-sitting weeks, I would head off from the office at 5 o'clock to a poker machine venue where I would have my first drink of the day whilst shoving money mindlessly into a cleverly designed machine. I would usually stay for an hour or an hour and a half and have a maximum of two glasses of wine. I was careful about the amount I drank because I was aware that I must not be picked up a second time for drink driving.

But the insidious poker machines were sucking me into

addiction. I had used them to blank out my mind as it filled with images and thoughts of horror that I could not bear. I would also use them to calm me if anything had startled me, even slightly. If a car came a bit close, or if I nearly tripped on the pavement I would be overwhelmed by panic, and rush to a poker machine venue to calm myself. I had been a psychologist and I knew how poker machines worked, but wish I had given more thought to what assailed me. It took me another four years to address that problem.

Meanwhile, what is the power of poker machines? When I was teaching learning theory to psychology students, I would use them as a powerful example of both classical and operant conditioning. On their own each of these learning tools can be controlling, so combined they are extraordinary. Classical conditioning is demonstrated by the old experiment with Pavlov and his dogs. He would present food and a sound almost simultaneously to his dogs. They would salivate at the sight and smell of the food and he would measure their salivation. After some time the dogs would salivate when they heard the sound only. Pairing the reward with the sound created a response to the sound as if it was the reward.

We are all at the pokies, 'salivating' at the bells, colours and music that accompany a win on the machines. Someone is winning something all the time in a poker machine venue, so bells, colour and music play constantly, and we are rewarded to some degree whether we are winning or not. It keeps us going.

The other reward-based learning is operant conditioning, which was demonstrated initially by psychologist, BF Skinner. He worked mainly with rats or pigeons. He demonstrated that a behaviour will increase if it is rewarded immediately after it is performed. His rats in a cage would press a lever more and more often when they received a reward for pressing it. They would find their way more quickly through a maze if they received a reward at the end than if they did not. Skinner worked on schedules of reward or reinforcement — he could reward the animal after every action, every 10, for example, or every five minutes. But he found the schedule that produced the wanted behaviour most often was an intermittent or unpredictable reward. This is exactly what poker machines offer.

❖

I began to feel concern about a need I seemed to be developing to go to the pokies even at times that I was not trying to escape horrible images, thoughts and feelings. *I can deal with this. I know all about these dammed things. I know how they work.*

On Wednesday 21 June 2006, a non-sitting week, I had been at my Ringwood office all day and at 5 o'clock went over to the Ringwood RSL for my couple of drinks and a play on the poker machines. Two things happened. First, I ran into someone I knew.

'Let me buy you a drink Carolyn.'

Bad idea. I was being social instead of thinking about the drinks. I bought my usual two glasses of wine on top of the one my acquaintance bought me.

Secondly I had decided that evening I would prove I could control the amount of money I put into the poker machines. I was concentrating on limiting my spending to $20. I probably stayed at the RSL for an hour and a half. I left the RSL feeling pleased that I could control my gambling. I forgot that I could only safely drink one glass of wine an hour.

I drove along Canterbury Road on the way home thinking I was clever. *I'm not addicted to gambling after all. I controlled it.* A cacophony of red and blue lights interrupted my self-congratulations. Apparently, the section Canterbury Road I was on is a well-known police booze bus trap. The road sweeps around a gentle bend revealing the breath testing station at the last minute. I flew into an immediate sick panic. *I have to kill myself. I can't live through this again.*

The ritual seemed familiar even though I had only been through it once before. I recall sitting in the police caravan. *I have to kill myself. I'll walk to the railway station, and throw myself under a train.* How did I dare have such thoughts, when I knew what my daughter's suicide had done to her daughter, her sisters and me. I was completely irrational with fear and panic. *My life is over.* The thoughts rolled round and round in my brain.

I did not leave the police caravan; I may have attempted to. *I know how Vicki felt when she killed herself.* I was locked in a black box from which there was no exit. *Perhaps I have to experience Vicki's feelings. That's why this has happened.* I never discovered how my friend Anne Eckstein arrived at the police caravan. I wish someone else had arrived because Anne held the most marginal seat in the state, and should not have been involved with my troubles. Anne drove me to the same private psychiatric hospital I had been in after I'd committed the previous misdemeanour, when I drove a car while my licence was suspended.

❖

I don't remember much of the next few weeks. I suppose I

had what is colloquially termed a 'nervous breakdown'. Over the last couple of years, I have read a number of newspaper clippings from the time. I gather the Premier was extremely angry — with just cause. Apparently the story of my second drink-driving offence in two years, and my third offence overall broke on the day the Premier was announcing a crackdown on P-plate drivers and drink-drivers. He told the media he had thrown me out of the Labor Party again. When asked if I would leave Parliament I think he said he did not care what I did, again understandably.

I actually remained in the Labor Party, because only the Administrative Committee of the Labor Party can dismiss a party member, after the matter has been to the disputes Tribunal. The Premier had not 'thrown me out' on the previous occasion either. I had given in to demands to sign a letter of resignation. However, I said nothing as I was not in a fit state to speak to the media.

I remained on sick leave until the election, and from time to time saw the same psychiatrist I had seen earlier. While my emotional state improved, I understand now that the improvements were superficial. It was as if a scab formed over an abscess that was still infected underneath. I actually thought over the next year that I did get better, and at some levels, I did.

❖

I had to attend court again in August, the Ringwood Court this time, and I received a penalty of 12 months licence suspension, a $600 fine and an order to undertake an alcohol education course. Apparently I was lucky. I could have been given a jail sentence for this offence. I think now that the severity of my actions still did not get through to me properly.

Press Statement following third lawbreaking episode

The psychiatrist I was seeing suggested I should do something that interested me.

'Here's a copy of 'Photoshop.' You should enroll in a course of digital photography that Rotary runs. Find an interest.'

I guess he thought I was being self-indulgent in persisting with my destructive behaviour. I was. He knew a lot about Borderline Personality Disorders, but not much about addiction or how to treat it.

I did not drink or gamble from the time of my third offence for almost a year. I decided I was cured of both addictions and would have no more worries in the future. How wrong I was.

❖

I understood the Premier's reaction to my repeated lawbreaking, the anger of many Labor Party Members and calls by the media and the public for my resignation from Parliament. My behaviour *was* reprehensible. At the same time, I did notice a comment in *The Age* a few weeks before my final offence, about the Premier's treatment of the member for Keilor, George Seitz.

Mr Bracks defended Mr Seitz, despite evidence from several ALP reviews on the extent of branch-stacking in the area. The party can disendorse Mr Seitz or force him to resign from the party and sit as an independent, as Mr Bracks did with left-aligned MP Carolyn Hirsh for drink driving in 2004.

"Carolyn Hirsh blows .07 and gets bounced. George Seitz makes hundreds of thousands of dollars go missing and the Premier backs him on the basis that the charges are not proven; it's ridiculous," a Left source said.

The Age Farrah Tomazin and Michael Bachelard: 16/05/2006

❖

I still have so much regret that I behaved in such a way to damage my colleagues electorally in marginal seats, and of course, the Labor Government. This is nothing compared with the remorse I feel for the hell I put my family through.

I also regret that I destroyed my reputation. Each time I broke the law, a barrage of media items followed, shredding my character into smaller pieces. I could not read, watch or listen to them for a long time. As well, since Andrew Olexander, the other Member for Silvan had a crash while driving at four times over the legal limit about six weeks after my first offence and six weeks before my second, we became interchangeable in some journalists' eyes. For example, Ellen Whinnett, a journalist with the Herald Sun, trashed my reputation even more than I deserved with one inaccurate sentence in an article on abortion law reform.

> "... *Removing abortion from the Crimes Act has been on the Labor Party's policy agenda for years, put there by the wider party but repeatedly ignored by the conservative, steady-as-she goes parliamentary party led by Bracks....*
>
> ...*Upper House MP Carolyn Hirsh planned to introduce a private member's Bill, but left Parliament after a drunken car crash before she could see the Bill through...*"
> Melbourne Herald Sun, July 21, 2007.

Perhaps when I had done so much to destroy myself, I should not whinge when someone distorts the truth to make my behaviour seem even worse than it was, but it didn't help. I have since learned that addiction is an illness, that it changes the brain, and it's hard work to change it back.

CHAPTER 19
'THE FULL BOGAN PACKAGE'
(Comment by John Faine ABC Radio 774 – 27/05/2011)

'Free breakfast.' I saw the sign outside a sprawling hotel each morning as I drove home after dropping my granddaughter at school in Glen Iris. It was early 2000 and Jessica was staying with me in Boronia while her mother spent time in hospital. School began at 8:30 am so we had an early start each weekday morning. I usually ate breakfast after I arrived home at about 9:15 am, but the sign was tempting. One morning I went in to investigate — into a *hotel* at 8.45 am. The sign spoke the truth. Tea and coffee, good coffee, fresh bread, white and wholemeal, butter, jam, vegemite and the morning papers, all set up in a lounge style alcove of the hotel. Free, no strings attached. An hour of peace and comfort — a buffer between the hectic start and the rest of the day. I took to breakfasting there most mornings. The breakfast alcove overlooked a spacious, bright area dominated by banks of poker machines — my personal introduction. I was to find out much later that there is no such thing as a free breakfast.

❖

I was familiar with poker machines in two ways. First, my brother and his family lived in Wodonga, and when I stayed there, we would cross the border into NSW, dine for five dollars at the Commercial Club, and entertain ourselves after dinner by putting two dollars each into a poker machine. I remember we laughed a lot and once won ten dollars!

My second involvement was as a member of Victoria's Labor Government, that introduced poker machines into Victoria in 1992. The then Premier, Joan Kirner, announced the policy in mid-1991, in answer to a question without notice. Her speech contained comment on extra jobs the new industry would create, both directly and indirectly, improved facilities   that poker machines would bring to Victoria's licensed clubs, and convenience for Victoria's pensioners, who were '...sick to death of having to travel on buses over the border every week to play the machines.' The statement also emphasised the strong controls that would be set in place to 'guarantee to the people of Victoria the cleanest as well as the best deal possible in the introduction of electronic gambling machines.' The legislation, allowing for 10,000 machines, was passed during that year, and the machines commenced operation in clubs and pubs in 1992, during the death throes of the Kirner Government. The Kennett Liberal Government was elected later that year, and soon after there were 30,000 poker machines in Victoria.

The President of the Knox Club, in my electorate, had lobbied me extensively to support the legislation, and I made a short speech in support during the second reading debate, using the standard spiel, including the pleasure pensioners would gain from playing machines at their local club, instead of having to traipse to NSW. This was the first irony.

The second irony was that I was the only speaker in the debate to refer at any length to the possible dangers of poker machines. I spoke about the fact that people with certain personality traits are more likely than others to become addicted to gambling, as they can to alcohol, nicotine and other drugs. I pointed out that as in the case with addictions to alcohol and nicotine, an addiction to gambling can have serious consequences.

The main reason for the introduction of the poker machine gambling industry into Victoria, aside from extraordinary lobbying by interest groups, like clubs, pubs and poker machine manufacturers, was its promise of a lucrative new tax base, essential given the parlous state of Victoria's finances at the time. Now, twenty years later, the state is so dependent on gaming revenue from poker machines (and Crown Casino), that they can't afford to close down the industry.

A horrifying statistic points out that '...revenue from gaming machines in pubs and clubs accounts for more than half of the $4 billion in gambling revenue collected by state governments in fiscal year 2002 – 03 in Australia.'

I have little doubt that a factor in John Cain's demise as Premier in 1990 was his vehement opposition to the introduction of a gambling industry. I believe that the 40 percent of poker machine players who are, or have been 'problem gamblers', that is, addicted to poker machines, including me, wish John Cain's position had prevailed in Victoria. John Cain knew about poker machines, as did many others. As early as 1974, a report from a Western Australian Royal Commission into gambling found that '...poker machine playing is a mindless, repetitive and insidious form of gambling which has many undesirable features. It requires no thought, no skill or social contact... Watching people playing the machines over long periods, the impressionistic evidence at least is that they are addictive to many people.'

❖

I enjoyed the routine of breakfasting in my little alcove at the pub, but my curiosity about the machines in front of me grew week by week. There was a scatter of people sitting in front of them, and none of them availed themselves of the free breakfast. They seemed engrossed, despite the appearance of the activity as a meaningless waste of time. To sit on a chair set at a suitable height, and continually press a button, watching four or five rolling reels eventually stopping in a predetermined pattern of pictures looked interminably boring. Each machine had its own theme, like ducks or Captain Marvel or fish. Every now and then, a cacophony of music and sound would peal from one of the machines — signaling a win, I learned.

After a couple of weeks, I decided to have a go at it. I recalled that ten years before, I had contributed one vote in favour of their introduction. I am disappointed I did not reread my contribution to the debate then, rather than ten years later. I might have left the machines alone. I put a couple of dollars in, and while the activity seemed pointless, I ended up with a couple of dollars more than ten minutes before. Was that the start of it?

From then, I added a fifteen minute or so sojourn on the

'pokies' most days after my breakfast. Sometimes I didn't have time, sometimes I lost up to five dollars, which was really too much, but sometimes I won a couple of dollars or so. Perhaps the real start of what became one of my two serious addictions was a morning I actually won fifty dollars. I could not believe it. No wonder they sat there engrossed in their machines. They wanted to win fifty dollars too, and I had shown myself it was possible.

I am not quite sure when my poker machine involvement moved from a harmless pastime to a full-blown addiction. It was not in 2000. I assume that as with the addiction I developed to alcohol, it was a gradual process; it crept up on me. I have no doubt that those free breakfasts eight years before introduced me to an activity, which, by the end of 2008 had become a dangerous addiction, almost destroying me financially, and even more horrifyingly, my family, who came to my aid.

I learned the power of poker machines as an aid to blocking emotion — they enabled me to hypnotise myself, to avoid guilt and grief over my daughter's suicide, and later public shame and humiliation that overwhelmed me. I tried to give myself an 'emotion replacement' and became one of the lonely individuals I had watched seven years before, when I had called in for my 'free' breakfast. Now *I* sat on a chair, adjusted for height, engrossed in the meaningless pursuit of shoving a great deal of money into a slot, in order to press a button repeatedly, in the hope that the next button press would reward me.

The Diagnostic and Statistical Manual of Mental Disorders (DSM4) published by the American Psychiatric Association describes the symptoms of a wide range of mental illnesses and disorders, to aid professionals in diagnosis. A set of ten symptoms, of which evidence of at least five in an individual leads to a diagnosis of pathological gambling is among them. I did not need the manual to tell me that by the end of 2008, I had at least five of those symptoms. First and most important, I gambled to escape, to improve my mood. Whenever a stressful event occurred, or guilt or grief over Vicki's death threatened to take me over, I rushed to the 'pokies' to block it all out. It worked too. I learned about the engrossing nature of these machines as they induced in me an altered state of consciousness. I understood why addicted poker machine players are completely engrossed in the machines until their money runs out. They are hypnotised. Others of the ten symptoms listed that I exhibited included a need to bet progressively more to experience the same state of peace, and a sense of panic whenever I would decide I would not go to the pokies again. I would need to rush off to the pokies for a 'fix' to deal with the panic. To hide my shame, and to my shame, I lied to family and friends about the extent of my gambling. Last and worst, as I seemed to be winning my war against this beast, I found myself in financial difficulties, from which, to my overwhelming gratitude alongside flooding shame and guilt, my hurt and puzzled family bailed me out.

I eventually contacted Gamblers' Help, who leave cards throughout poker machine venues, and over two years of involvement with them, I almost ceased gambling. Gamblers' Help is funded from the ubiquitous Community Support Fund, to which some of Victoria's gambling tax revenue is directed. It is an excellent organisation, and helped me a great deal in overcoming the addiction.

However, as I gradually overcame my addiction to poker machines throughout 2009, another problem, addiction to alcohol, came to the fore.

❖

It took me a long time to reach an answer that satisfied me as to why I developed an addiction to poker machines. I have never been interested in other forms of gambling. My grandmother loved the horses, and was a skilled punter. Her TAB phone account gave her a regular small income boost. I became familiar with this form of gambling after she lost her sight at the age of eighty-six. I used to go to her house each Saturday morning to read the form guide to her and ring her bets through. She rang me the day before her death to tell me of a good win, but the pastime never interested me

I have no doubt that I have a genetic predisposition to addiction. As well as my father, other members of his family were alcoholics, and some of my mother's family were 'drinkers', not referred to as alcoholics. Of course I had been addicted to cigarettes. But poker machines? As I recover, thoughts of, 'how could I?' and 'why did I,' run around my brain on occasion. There is some evidence that playing poker machines has much in common with addictive drugs, like cocaine. Both work by hijacking the brain's pleasure centres — a lure that some people cannot resist, in the end, physiologically. Perhaps that was the case, or perhaps grief and guilt about my daughter's death washed away my willpower. Another explanation for me is that gambling with poker machines was an attempt to apply a lesson I learned from my hip and knee replacements. Use a mechanical replacement and you will be better.

❖

During 2009, while I attended counselling with the Gamblers Help organisation, I hardly played 'the pokies', but I substituted that activity with alcohol. I would look at my watch every few minutes from about four o'clock each day. *Only an hour to go till I can have a drink, only forty-three minutes to wait.* I continued the lie to myself that I could not be an alcoholic because I did not drink before five in the afternoon each day. Every night for most of 2009, and most nights the previous year, I drank, and the amount slowly increased. Drinking was like poker machine gambling. I kept on needing more to get the same satisfaction. I was engaged in a dance in which poker machines and alcohol wove intricate patterns in my brain — they seemed to have a symbiotic relationship.

❖

Wine had been part of my life for many years, and had once included a diverse cellar of excellent reds and whites. When dinner guests came, I would search, knowledgeably, for a suitable bottle, and there would always be something pleasant to take to meals out. Wine drinking was intermittent, social and only in company. Observation of my alcoholic father and a mantra from my mother had taught me, *never drink alone. Only alcoholics drink alone.*

Two roads led me to solitary drinking, and to alcoholism. The first was after Jess and I moved to Glen Iris, at about the time of Vicki's death in 2001. I shared a glass of wine with myself as I prepared dinner. After a while, I followed it with a glass with dinner, then a glass while packing the dishes. This gradually became a habit. A bottle from my cellar lasted two nights.

After I was elected at the end of 2002, the habit asserted itself even when I was not at home preparing dinner. Around five most evenings, if the House was to sit after dinner, I would pop around to the bar with a colleague or two for a glass of wine, and I would have a second glass with dinner. While I largely modelled my job description and work habits on my previous time in Parliament, this road was one I had not travelled before. I do not believe that I would have been classified 'alcoholic' at this stage, although there is no doubt the alcohol-welcoming receptors in my brain would rub their hands together in anticipation around five o'clock each day. Warning signs were there, but if I noticed them I ignored them.

Poker machines had provided me with another avenue for solitary drinking. For me, 'playing the pokies' was an occupation I engaged in on my own, and in the evenings I accompanied it with two to three glasses of wine, depending how long I stayed at the venue. During this time, my taste in wine deteriorated. *Why spend money on expensive wine when you can slide it into a machine, and perhaps win?* I almost had to hold my nose to get down the first mouthful of vinegary 'house chardy'.

❖

As I continued counselling with 'gamblers help' throughout 2009, I put on ten kilograms. I almost stopped gambling — I reduced my excursions to poker machine venues to about once a month, but concentrated on buying the cheapest casks of wine I could buy — four litres of fresh dry white from Aldi for $8.95, which I drank at home in the evenings. Particularly frightening, each cask was only lasting for four nights. Measurement was never my strong point at school, but I could not help working out the total — a litre a night.

Avoiding the medical consequences of my behaviour was easy. I phoned whichever doctor I was due to see, cancelled the appointment, and did not make another one. That way I flew below the medical radar. I didn't know what was going on inside my body, and I did not intend to allow anyone else to find out. I ignored the bathroom scales, although I could not ignore the sneaky retrieval of my very big clothes, or my aching knees.

I sometimes pictured my blood running with sugar, arteries dammed — or damned, by cholesterol, liver doubled in size and kidneys on their last legs. I thought of my brain, synapses opening tributaries for the overflow of wine. But, generally I felt alright, especially from five o'clock onwards. Not so good after three or four hours of dreamless sleep. Not so good the next morning. I was not sure how much of each night was sleep, and how much alcoholic oblivion. I thought I might drink myself to death and I did not care.

❖

During three days at Inverloch with my two daughters and their families, during the January holidays, I behaved as usual on two nights of the three. The middle night I only had three drinks and went to bed early. I felt quite virtuous. My daughters bandied around the word 'drunk' accusingly and regularly. My two sons-in-law kept their mouths shut, to me. But I found out later that one had told his wife I must not mind their children any more.

'You were very funny,' my daughters said. 'But you were drunk, pissed!'

I didn't say much. 'I wasn't too bad, I had a few drinks, sure, but it was a holiday.'

'Mum, I had to hold your arm and take you back to your cabin. You couldn't walk straight.'

'I don't think that was the case,' I said.

'Mum, you can't remember most of the evening. You'll die if you keep drinking like this. We don't want you to die. Please do something. Please go to a doctor.'

Her last words finally wriggled their way into my alcohol laced brain, and I was mortified. I hadn't realised they could tell I'd had too much to drink. But it was true and I admitted to myself at last that I had not been able to remember much of the previous evening. In fact there had been many occasions when I had not been able to remember much of previous evenings. Sometimes it would be half past nine, and I would crawl into bed, astonished that it was two o'clock.

I went to a doctor. Had tests. Not as bad as I had thought, but diabetes now, rather than pre-diabetes. My daughter's words kept ringing in my ears. *We don't want you to die. Please do something. Please go to a doctor.*

Did I want to die? Heavy drinking meant I did not have to address the question. If I kept going, there was no doubt I would die, just as my father had. A tiny glimmer of sanity trickled through the alcohol pooling through my body. I did not want to put my family through the pain of my early death when they had already lost so much.

Another gleam of light appeared. I had joined a local writing group in 2007, at the behest of a friend, and this led me to undertake some short writing courses and enrollment in a

Diploma of Professional Writing and Editing. More questions arose. If I felt like a fur-covered headache until about eleven o'clock each morning, and wrote myself off with cheap wine instead of a pen from five each evening, when would I write? And if I kept drinking the way I was, my brain would end up too addled for me to write. I had to decide. Living required me to heal my wounds. I had to stop pasting over festering sores of grief, guilt and shame with wine. I had to pick off the scabs covering the rotten flesh and allow the sun and air to flow through them.

I acknowledged at last that I was no longer the 'normal' social drinker I used to be, but had become a full-blown alcoholic, the same as my father, of whom I had been so ashamed.

I made an appointment with an addiction specialist. I sat in his room and wept for an hour, berating myself for being a hopeless failure. He wanted me to enter a program — a week of detoxification and four weeks of rehabilitation.

'No, I want to keep up with the writing course I've started,' I said.

Writing felt like a gossamer thread attaching me to hope. I did not want to let it go.

'What about alcoholics anonymous? (AA) It might work for you,' he suggested.

I made a choice and agreed to try it.

I went to meetings, day after day for six months, hearing stories and telling mine. I did not drink, but sipped at words — formed them into fluid sentences that flowed through my brain. Each morning a screen-full of words greeted me, and I added more.

I found AA interesting, and comforting. It had a twelve-step program — the first step was an admission of powerlessness over alcohol. I managed that — after all, that was why I went to AA. However, the second step flummoxed me. It required belief in a Higher Power, which was necessary for recovery. This seemed to mean religion, which I had given up forty-five years earlier, and I had no desire to revisit the Presbyterian church of my early years. I thought about it a lot, but ran into this impermeable barrier all the time.

Meanwhile, after a couple of months without drinking, the other half of my addiction, that I believed I had beaten, reappeared. I started gambling again — I was not cured. I was caught in a web of what Jon Faine on the ABC lightly termed, 'the full bogan package.'

I was back where I had been two years before, so after six months I stopped attending AA meetings and began drinking again as well as gambling, hope trickling and clinking away.

CHAPTER 20

A LONG WAY BACK

It took me 10 years to be able to stand still with many memories of the half-open doorway of the garage at Vicki's house and look at her hanging from a rafter by a rope around her neck; to look carefully at the kitchen stool lying on the cracked concrete floor; to contemplate the shoe that had fallen from her foot. I finally found the courage to grieve for my lost daughter, to cast aside the horror and guilt, and find and feel the core of my sadness. I have stopped asking *Why? What did I do wrong? Could I have prevented her death?* I simply miss the beautiful person she was behind her illness. I have forgiven myself, and I have forgiven Vicki.

Flemington racecourse looks magnificent in early spring. Thousands of roses are covered in buds ready for a spectacular display on Melbourne Cup day. My roses should be in full bloom at the same time. I planted roses in my new garden during its first winter, including *Peace*, *Just Joey* and *Blue Moon*.

These three were among the roses I had grown in Boronia, where I lived in the 1990s for seven years after I sold the family home in Bayswater. At Bayswater, we had a low-maintenance native garden that included gum trees, acacias, lots of grevilleas and bottlebrush. The Boronia house was a post World War II style, and once my renovations that kept it in character were complete, I indulged myself by planning an old-fashioned garden. I think with the family grown I wanted to recreate my grandmother's garden, a garden of cameos from my early childhood. In Boronia, I had a magnolia tree, camellias, fuchsias, dahlias in autumn, a carpet of violets and an abundance of roses.

New garden — new life

My son-in-law Geoff, landscape gardener by trade, shaped the builder's site around my new house into a delightful garden, while I was away finally facing my demons. I experience pleasure in my garden, the pleasure that for a while, I could only experience while I was drinking or playing poker machines.

I nurture those feelings as I select and plant, feed and weed. Whenever joy and pleasure flood into my awareness, as they do more often nowadays, they overwhelm me. I believed I had lost those feelings for good.

❖

I went back to see the addiction specialist I had seen earlier in the year, associate Prof Alan Gijsbers, and this time I paid proper attention to what he said and to my own despair. Dr Gijsbers has an impressive set of qualifications and is the Medical Director (Addiction Medicine Service at the Royal Melbourne Hospital) and Medical Director (Substance Withdrawal Unit at The Melbourne Clinic). The Melbourne Clinic runs a substance withdrawal program and a rehabilitation program. I took a major step and admitted myself to these programs. A combination of highly qualified staff and well-structured programs meant I took my first steps along the path to health. Following the five-week program, I continued with professional support, both through the clinic and privately, with regular visits to a psychologist. I tinker around the edges of spirituality, and find comfort in the concept of something beyond myself.

I ask myself whether, had I seriously sought help earlier, I could have avoided the shame and humiliation of the last few years, and decide that it is possible, or not. There's no point dwelling on it. The first steps of my recovery were to finally face Vicki's suicide and my complicity in it, without blaming myself. Somewhere within me had lived a primitive belief that I had murdered her. *All my fault, deserve to be punished.* I had to shake the guilt away and simply, grieve.

'What are you feeling? Right here? Right now?' the therapist would ask.

Same answer every time. 'Grief, guilt, shame.'

My journey along that jagged section of road is well past now. The feelings when I look back over the past ten, twenty, fifty or seventy years are sometimes of sadness and regret, but also joy and pleasure, and laughter.

For example, I have written about how awful it was living at Cressy as a child, but as I unpacked the last dusty carton of the hundred or so boxes of books I lugged from house to house for ten years, a delightful image floated into my mind. The faded label on this last box said *Children's Books*. Yes, there was Enid Blyton — *The Famous Five*: Julian, Dick, Ann, George and Timmy the dog.

I am ten years old, sitting with my feet in the oven of the wood stove in the kitchen at Cressy, reading. It is the May holidays and winter has come. I am lost in a story where our dog Tippy is Timmy, and my father does not come home drunk every night. These children are magic. I become George, the tomboy, really Georgina, but she hates it. Ann is a simpering girl of the nineteen forties. I want to be George. I am George while I read, book after book. My mother takes me on the bus to the library in Colac to borrow enough books to last the holidays. The rain pelts on our corrugated iron roof. I poke another raw edged lump of red gum into the stove. I shove it well back with the sooty poker. Shut the firebox door, feet back in the warm oven. I am back on Kerrin Island with the Famous Five.

'Watch the shop while I get the tea done Carolyn.' My mother wants the kitchen.

My brothers Alan and Kevin, and Tippy the Border Collie bounce in, wet, stinking and hungry. I escape through the dining room to the shop, grab a chocolate frog from the glass lolly case, and become George again.

❖

I kept asking myself how the last ten years happened. Dr Gijsbers pointed out that mind-altering drugs, such as alcohol — and I believe poker machines, which, while not drugs, behave the same way — perform two important functions. First, they fire up the pleasure centre of the brain. Their second function is to act as an anaesthetic, eloquently described in a 1953 quote by Aldous Huxley, which states '... The need for chemical vacations from intolerable self-hood and repulsive environments will undoubtedly remain...'

I also remembered a Canadian psychologist I studied during psychology lectures at Monash in the 1970s. Donald Hebb wrote a seminal book, *The Organisation of Behaviour*, (1949), in which he combined theories of that time about behaviour and the brain to propose a new theory — that neurons stimulated together will join together. His theory, known as Hebb's Law, is paraphrased as *neurons that fire together wire together*. If alcohol, or poker machine gambling, or other drugs regularly stimulate the pleasure centres of the brain, then those pleasure neurons will join up with the neurons undertaking the activity. The neurons driving activities that were once paired with the brain's pleasure centres shrivel and die.

I had to rewire my brain, to reconnect my brain's pleasure centres with activities that are truly pleasurable, like my grandchildren's laughter, my roses, the wind on my face as I pedalled my bicycle, and the sheer pleasure of living.

I thought Vicki's illness of a borderline personality disorder created the most self-centred behaviour imaginable, but I now believe the illness of addiction comes close, as addiction manifests itself as an endless pursuit of immediate pleasure and immediate anaesthetizing, irrespective of the long-term consequences to the self or others.

Early in my recovery, I wrote a series of poems about Vicki, and I reproduce one of them here.

Memories of Laughter

I look for you in the black corners, always the memory of your last presence

a bundle of clothes swaying darkly.

I look for you on the streets with your head high

your hand gently holding your daughter's small one

your laughter flying skywards.

I can tell you've been present when I see your glorious daughter

living, loving, laughing, crying.

I think I once saw you in a dream, alive, vibrant, laughing still.

Now you lie, sharing a space with your father

a bowl of ashes beneath the sticky clay.

❖

The road of recovery has been rocky. I can still see it stretching ahead, so far that sometimes it seems like a mirage, but often as I experience pleasure and laughter, I know my brain is slowly rewiring itself. The secret is to concentrate on the steps I take each moment, to make them deliberate and firm, and to turn them into a dance whenever possible.

POLITICS, DEATH & ADDICTION

CAROLYN HIRSH

		Qty
ISBN 9781922175458		
RRP	AU19.99	.....
Postage within Australia	AU$5.00	.....
	TOTAL★ $_____	

★ All prices include GST

Name:..

Address: ....

....

Phone:...

Email: ....

Payment: ❏ Money Order ❏ Cheque ❏ MasterCard ❏Visa

Cardholders Name:...

Credit Card Number: ....

Signature:...

Expiry Date: ....

Allow 7 days for delivery.

Payment to: Marzocco Consultancy (ABN 14 067 257 390)
                   PO Box 12544
                   A'Beckett Street, Melbourne, 8006
                   Victoria, Australia
                   admin@brolgapublishing.com.au

CL111801